THE HERAI
DIARY

THE HERALD DIARY

Beyond Compare

Ken Smith

BLACK & WHITE PUBLISHING

First published 2012
by Black & White Publishing Ltd
29 Ocean Drive, Edinburgh EH6 6JL

1 3 5 7 9 10 8 6 4 2   12 13 14 15

ISBN: 978 1 84502 487 1

Typeset by Ellipsis Digital Limited, Glasgow
Printed and bound by MPG Books Ltd, Bodmin

Contents

Introduction

Who would make fun of Rangers Football Club, politicians, students, and the weather? Well Scots would, and then they would send the funniest stories, gossip and overheard gems to the Diary column in *The Herald* newspaper.

This is the best of these yarns and gags from over the year, gathered together in the one volume.

If you want to know what makes Scots laugh, and have a smile yourself, then look no further.

1
Having Your Cake

Scotland's shops are under pressure from the recession and online buying. But clicking a computer will never give you the joy of meeting folk at the shops.

WE HEAR about a man being grilled by a Partick supermarket security guard who claimed the shopper had put something in his backpack.

Iain Todd tells us the guard looked in the bag and asked why it was lined with tinfoil – a common ruse to block security tag signals.

The man responded with admirable sangfroid. "Someone," he says indignantly, "has stolen my roast chicken!"

SHOPPERS were looking for bargains after Christmas. One woman in the Waitrose supermarket in Newton Mearns spotted a fellow shopper heading to the checkout carrying a turkey, and she wondered if they were on sale.

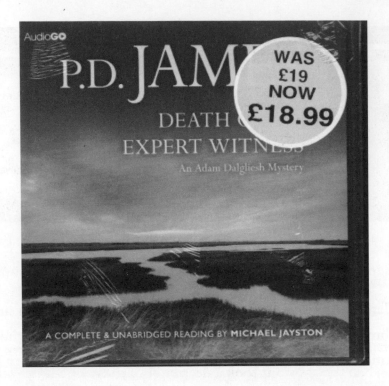

She went up to the chap and asked: "Are they going cheap?" "No," he replied. "They're all dead."

A GLASGOW reader tells us he visited his late-night corner store where he asked the salesperson what time they closed.

"We close at 10 o' clock," the woman replied. "But we start giving dirty looks at a quarter to."

IN THE aftermath of the gales, it was natural that some folk would take the mickey. An English chap visiting Scotland told us: "I think there's been panic buying in Scotland because of the extreme weather.

GU Mini
Puds/Cheesecake/Saucy Pots 3x45g

1/2 price

£2.39
£2

£1.49 per 100g
Offer ends 16th September

I was in five supermarkets in Lanarkshire and couldn't find any fresh fruit or vegetables in any of them."

JUDE MACLAVERTY was buying a muffin in a Glasgow coffee shop when the assistant took a deep sniff of the cake before putting it in a bag.

After savouring her sniff she proudly announced to a startled Jude: "Ah've had a gastric band fitted – that's the closest Ah get tae cakes these days."

"I'M ON the waiting list for a new kidney," the chap excitedly announced to his pals in a Glasgow pub.

"That's some exclusive butcher's you use," replied his impassive mate.

STRANGE customer requests – assistant Anne Morrison in Glasgow sports emporium, Greaves, was asked by a customer if they stocked football pumps with needle adaptors.

When she confirmed they did, he asked if he could borrow one. Not expecting a game to kick off in the store, she asked why he merely

wished a temporary loan, and he replied that he wished to clean out the wax in his hearing aid.

Alas his request fell on deaf ears.

AN EDINBURGH reader tells us she was in a smart Stockbridge deli when a young chap asked: "Do you sell whales' eggs?" The assistant thought about this briefly before asking: "Do you mean quails' eggs?" There was an even longer pause before the potential customer answered: "Maybe."

MORE and more bargain-seeking shoppers are venturing in to the more cheap and cheerful type of supermarket, but they still take a bit of getting used to. Reader Jim Clark tells us: "Going round the Perth branch of Lidl recently, I couldn't help hearing a posh middle-aged woman say to her elderly parent, 'I don't think this is a Dubonnet sort of place, Daddy.'"

AN AYRSHIRE reader tells us he came out of his local supermarket to see a woman unable to control her full trolley on a slight slope when it ran away from her and crashed into the back of his car.

He quickened his pace and shouted over to her: "Any damage?" "Maybe a couple of eggs cracked," she told him.

GUS FURRIE in East Kilbride tells us that his daughter was working nightshift in a local petrol station when a chap came in looking to buy cigarettes. Says Gus: "He looked under 18 so she asked him for some ID.

"He said he had none, and then in a flash of inspiration said he had a tattoo, which by law you have to be 18 to get.

"He then showed her what was clearly a home-made tattoo, so no ciggies there then."

HOLIDAY time, and a number of people are buying their summer clothes. A Glasgow reader heard a girl in the changing rooms struggling into skintight jeans tell her pal: "I think they're too tight," then added: "If I was being chased I widnae be able to run. I could wind up deid."

"Aye, but at least you'd look good," consoled her friend.

IT CAN be a stressful time ordering coffees with all their different names. A reader was in a Glasgow coffee shop when the barista shouted out: "I have a tea, latte, and cappuccino."

No-one moved to collect them until the chap serving stared at the customer at the front of the queue who eventually replied: "No, not mine. I ordered a latte, cappuccino, and tea."

A READER tells us he was in a city centre newsagents when a wee wifey brought in a packet of batteries, and said she wanted to return them.

When the shopkeeper asked what was wrong with them she said they had only worked for a few weeks, yet it said on the side they would not expire until 2014.

AN AYRSHIRE golf club member tells us the chaps in the bar were discussing how their parents had a more laissez-faire attitude to parenting than perhaps happens today. One chap recalled that when his dad took him to the supermarket he would leave him in the aisle with the comics and collect him when the shopping was done.

One Saturday this happened as usual, but when they got home his mother revealed that his dad had actually come home without him until she asked where their son was, and dad realised he was still reading the comics and quickly returned to the shop.

EVEN CHEMISTS can have a sense of humour. A Glasgow reader waiting for his prescription heard a young woman, who was scratching her pink arm, ask the pharmacist: "What's best for nasty insect bites?"

"Probably midges," he replied.

IT'S BEEN a while since we mentioned the great Dundee record store Groucho's and its collection of daft conversations between staff and customers who are not always on the ball. Like the customer who couldn't find what he wanted and asked if there were any other record shops around.

"HMV," replied the assistant. "How do you spell that?" asked the customer.

GROUCHO'S also sells concert tickets, which is why a customer once asked: "What time is The Damned gig?"

"The doors open at half past eight," said the assistant.

"Are The Doors playing as well?" asked the surprised customer.

SOME conversations are just plain daft. We hear of the woman in the Glasgow corner shop who asked: "Do you sell Elastoplast?"

When the shopkeeper said "What?" the customer repeated her need for Elastoplast and the shopkeeper said: "Oh, I thought you said something about 'the last of the Apaches.'"

"That film was called *The Last of the Mohicans*," said the customer, trying to be helpful.

Now thoroughly confused, the shopkeeper replied: "What film?"

WE DON'T know what the demand is, but cheap-products emporium Poundland in Airdrie is selling tins of yacht varnish with a nifty picture of a ship's wheel on the front. A reader who was pondering whether Airdrie was now the Riviera of Monklands was interrupted by a fellow customer who opined: "The only Marina I know around here works in the chip shop."

HAVE YOU seen these folk who meander the streets sipping out of fancy coffee cups? Kirsty Buchanan was in a bargain emporium in Glasgow when her partner picked up a thermal cup in the gadget section and turned it over to see the price tag on the bottom.

Recounts Kirsty: " When he turned it over, coffee came out, and only then did he notice the guy standing next to him staring at him – it was his coffee.

"He had just that second put it down to look at something and was a little surprised at the stranger who had apparently walked over to pour his coffee on the floor."

A READER in a Glasgow clothing store waiting to buy an item watched as the chap in front handed over two £20 notes for a £30 jumper and had to wait while the assistant ostentatiously passed them under a UV light sensor on her desk to check they weren't fakes.

Then when she handed the chap a £10 note in change he leaned over the desk, and ran it under the same UV light before putting it in his pocket.

A YOUNG Glasgow chap was heard telling his pal, who asked how his hotel evening job was going, that he had got off with a warning when a guest came up to the desk and asked: "Excuse me, but I've forgotten what room I'm in."

"That's OK sir," the young chap had replied. "You're in the hotel lobby."

A CHAP in Partick was telling his pal: "I was in Blockbusters, and you can get huge bags o' sweets with yer films."

His mate thought about this before asking: "Who would want to rent a bag o' Maltesers?"

IT'S GREAT to see the new Morrison's supermarket in Glasgow's east end bringing an abundance of fruit and veg to the area, but there are some teething problems.

Andy Cumming was impressed by the big range of tomatoes, and took a couple of plum tomatoes and a handful of cherry tomatoes to the checkout. The young chap at the till hesitated before ringing them up, and asked what varieties he had. Andy replied: "Plum and cherry."

"You're at it mate," the chap replied. "I know a tomato when I see it."

LESLEY FALCONER was at her east end hairdresser in Glasgow when a local came in for a chat and told the hairdresser she had spotted her at a funeral the previous week.

Recalling the occasion, the hairdresser commented: "When I go, I'm going to have a funeral like that, with a humanist."

The local lady seemed a bit puzzled before she replied: "I didn't think he was that funny."

DAFT LINE of the week – a girl came out of a Glasgow store and told her pal: "I almost wet myself when I read what someone had written on a door in there."

"What was it?" said her pal, an expectant smile already forming on her lips.

"Toilet closed," she replied.

Civilian Marmalade
Oranges

AH, the humour of the newsagent's. Donald Macaskill was buying his *Herald* in the west end when the chap behind the counter asked: "Who are you backing to win?" He was pointing at the *Herald* headline: "David Hayman plays King Lear."

CHARLIE ANDREWS in Greenock tells us his pal was in the 10 items or fewer queue at his local supermarket and could see that a woman further up the queue had a full trolley groaning with groceries. Says Charlie: "None of the other shoppers complained but my pal's blood pressure was rising. The cashier beckoned the woman to come forward looked into the trolley and asked sweetly, 'So which 10 items would you like to buy?'

"Blood pressure back to normal instantly."

A SHOPPER in a cheap and cheerful store in Sauchiehall Street heard the old lady next to him show a handbag she was considering purchasing to her pal and tell her: "It's just right. It's got two ootside pockets – wan fur ma phone, and wan fur ma teeth."

"You never see that mentioned in the Mulberry adverts," says our shopper.

WHEN THE SALES were on, a reader overheard a trendy young man in Glasgow's city centre telling his girlfriend who was holding up a garish shirt for him to consider purchasing: "I don't know. Are you sure people would know I was wearing it ironically?"

A READER tells us he was in a pet shop when a youngster came in and pestered his mum to let him have a pet mouse. His mother was resisting, and told him: "Billy would end up eating it."

"Is that your cat?" asked the shop-owner.

"No, my brother," replied the little one.

2
Work It Out

As work becomes more stressful, the only answer it seems, is to have a laugh.

A MILNGAVIE reader swears that he had a handyman fixing some loose tiles on his roof who came down from his ladder and said he would have to go home early as he was feeling a bit dizzy.

"Vertigo?" asked our reader. "No, not far from the town centre," replied the handyman.

WE HEAR of a Glasgow office where the boss was organising a large conference, and sent a member of staff to buy a bundle of the little plastic sticks for folk to stir the cups of coffee they would be offered. Arriving in a supermarket the chap asked a member of staff: "I'm looking for these things for stirring coffee, but I don't know what they're called."

The staff member looked at him curiously, then slowly said: "Teaspoons."

A FORMER student, going for his latest job interview, later told his pals in a Byres Road pub: "My dad told me to make a really good first impression.

"So I wasn't sure whether to open with my Sean Connery or my Frank Spencer."

A BORDERS businessman tells us his secretary, who was pregnant, was going for a scan, as there was the possibility of twins. When she returned to work he asked how the scan had gone.

"Fine, jist the yin," she replied. "And the sex?" he asked, knowing that she was keen on a daughter.

"Oh aye, he says Ah can do it fur a bit yet," came her unexpected answer.

GOVERNMENT changes to the benefits system are forcing more people to apply for jobs they don't really want in order to keep their benefits. We hear of one Glasgow chap at an interview who was asked if he drank.

"Thanks," he replied, "but I'd rather wait until the interview's over."

OH TO BE young and on your first job. An East Kilbride reader reveals: "My young niece working for the first time behind a bar in London was asked for a lager and lime. She handed the customer a glass of lager, a lime, and a knife. Needless to say that was her last shift."

GLASGOW innovation manager Grant Gibson was at a meeting where the helpful instructor announced: "You can ask me anything. I'm a minefield of information."

Grant was too nervous to ask her anything in case she blew up.

A GLASGOW reader tells us a work colleague impressed him when he had to make a presentation to the rest of the staff about the project on which he had been working. His opening words to the assembled audience was: "The boss told me to start with a joke." He then projected a picture onto the screen of his wage slip.

MORE FOLK are taking sandwiches to work for their lunch to save money. It reminds us of the Glasgow chap who told us: "There's a strange thing happening in the office kitchen just now – folk are putting names on food in the fridge.

"Yesterday I had a tuna sandwich called Marilyn."

THE NEWS story about the woman who allegedly poisoned her milk at work to stop people stealing it reminds Raymond Lowe of when he worked at Babcock's. "I would take a two-pound bag of sugar in on a Monday and when I came in on a Tuesday, the bag was always empty. It was always thought they spent the nightshift making tablet," he tells us.

TALES of protecting foodstuffs remind Ian Allingham: "My dad was interned in Siam during the Second World War by the Japanese in a house which was serviced by a house boy.

"The internees noticed that the level of sherry in the decanter kept falling and one of them decided to replace half of the sherry with his own bodily fluid.

"This did not reduce the incidence of disappearing sherry so, after a few days, they confronted the house boy who explained that he was teetotal, but did regularly use the sherry as an ingredient when cooking their evening meals."

OUR MENTION of workplace food reminds Jim Scott: "When I worked in Shettleston we used to have a cook on the back shift who always had a cigarette in her mouth.

"One night I had a fried egg roll and my mate asked for 'the same but without the black pepper', only to be told 'it's no black pepper.'"

WORKPLACE eating continued. Frances Woodward in Mirfield, Yorkshire, recalls: "I had a temporary job with a company that supplied foodstuffs.

"If a pallet got damaged, it got written off and the stuff on it distributed amongst us. One day, the manager asked if any cans of lemonade were left. Apparently not. 'That's a shame,' he said.

"A resounding crash heard in the warehouse was followed by a cry of 'There is now', as a pallet accidentally fell off the forklift."

MATT VALLANCE recalls as a young man working in a Yorkshire tyre depot he was warned that under no circumstances was he to use the stainless steel bucket kept in a cupboard.

Says Matt: "I wondered why, until a Guinness tanker came in to have tyres fitted. Out came the bucket, round to the big hose connection at the back. When we finished that lunchtime it was Guinness all round."

"A LARGE roll of bubble wrap arrived in the office and I asked the boss what to do with it," said the young office assistant.

"He said, 'Just pop it in the corner.'

"Took me two hours."

"REVISIT your youth of ringing doorbells and running away," says a frustrated reader who stayed in for a delivery, "by becoming a Royal Mail delivery driver."

A FORMER colleague, now a freelance worker, told us: "Bank holiday Monday – or as we self-employed call it – Monday."

BOB GARDNER tells us his pal is a great cricket fan, and has the stack of three mail trays on his office desk labelled "In" "Out" and "LBW."

When anyone asks what LBW stands for, he tells them: "Let the b****** wait."

TEN YEARS after his death, a collection of writings by the legendary *Herald* editor Arnold Kemp has been published. Although folk remember him as a statesmanlike editor, he was far cheekier in his younger days. As a young journalist on the *Scotsman*, he and some colleagues spooked the night news editor with a fake wire story sent down the tubes saying that a flying saucer had landed at Buckingham Palace.

Much to their consternation, the night editor cleared the front page for the story. To stop him, Arnold then sent a fake D Notice from the Government stating that the story had to be kept secret.

POTENTIAL jobs were being discussed in a Glasgow pub when one toper opined: "Prison guard sounds a pretty easy job."

When asked for an explanation, he added: "I mean, who would try to steal a prison?"

A GLASGOW businessman tells us that writing negative references for former employees is no longer allowed at his company, for fear of being sued.

He felt though that he had got round the problem when he was asked for his opinion on a worker who constantly skived off before being shown the door. "A man like him is hard to find," he eventually stated.

OUR STORY of subtly negative references reminds Doug Griffin: "Many years ago, when I worked in East Kilbride, I heard about a pharmacist who worked in Boots and was a bit keen to get rid of a young boy who worked for him. He gave him a reference that said 'he dispensed with accuracy.'"

THE STORIES of ambiguous references lead to Ian Hutchison remarking: "I was reminded of the one which I have always enjoyed. 'He came fired with enthusiasm, and that is how he went.'"

AMBIGUOUS references continued. Says Adam Muir in Kirkintilloch: "While employed in local government I was persuaded to start a particular gent who turned out to be a less than ideal employee. Before his jotters were processed, he opted to leave but I was surprised when he turned up shortly after to request a reference.

"He left beaming, clutching a reference which read, 'Mr X was employed under my direction for a period of four months. During this period he carried out his duties to his utmost satisfaction.'"

MORE on references. Mairead Bloom tells us: "We worked in Zambia where the employment of servants was an important strand of the local economy.

"Most were excellent polymaths who kept expatriate families sane. One came to us shortly after we arrived with the reference, 'Kingston did us regularly and, given the chance, he will do you.'"

EVER BEEN SENT on a meaningless training course? A reader tells us about a colleague who was sent on such a tedious day out which under the new management-speak had been labelled as a 'workshop'. So while all the other attendees arrived in their business suits – it was for accounts staff after all – he instead turned up in a boiler suit and told the gobsmacked trainer: "I didn't want to get my good suit messed up in some dirty workshop."

BOBBY HOWIE saw an advert on S1 Jobs – "Fencer (Temporary) (2 posts)," it read. With just two posts, pretty temporary, then, suggests Bobby.

REFERENCES continued. Celia Stevenson tells us: "I have an American friend who, if he has to give a reference for a less than satisfactory employee, writes, 'If you can get X to work for your company, you will indeed be fortunate.'"

A RECRUITMENT consultant in Strathaven tells us he was pleased that a CV from a young chap included the fact he had achieved a Duke of Edinburgh Award as it showed his commitment. The consultant's enthusiasm was only tempered by the fact that the chap had written it as "Juke".

JIM SCOTT shakes his head as he tells us about the office assistant who queried how to type an address. He looked at it and said the person had put their street number in Roman numerals.

"But my computer doesn't have Roman numerals," she wailed.

WE MENTIONED mail trays on office desks, and Hugh Gibson in Crieff recalls a former colleague who had one on either side of his desk. One read "Ta" and the other "Ta-ta".

IN A GLASGOW company canteen, a worker told his colleagues: "I read recently that most companies deliberately employ one useless, incompetent, talentless idiot, just to boost office morale, focus the other employees and divert attention away from any management failings.

"What rubbish! I've looked around the whole office, and none of you fit that description."

JOB INTERVIEWS again, and a chap in human resources in Edinburgh claims he was interviewing one young chap and asked him: "What would you say your strengths are?" "Arms and back" the admittedly fit young man replied.

3
The Psychic Girlfriend

The course of true love isn't always a straight one. Here are some of the detours it takes.

GLASWEGIANS are so romantic, thought a reader from Maryhill catching the bus into town. Two women were discussing the sudden death of a mutual friend's husband. Discussing how bad it must be for their friend, one of them opined: "They were only married fur three year – so she probably still loved him."

READER Jim Fitzpatrick hears a chap in the pub declare: "It said in the wife's magazine that you burn as many calories having sex as you do in running a mile."

"Who can run a mile in 30 seconds?" came a voice from further up the bar.

ACTUALLY that reminds us of a conversation we heard in an Ashton Lane pub. A young woman was explaining to her pals about the latest disaster in her love life when a less than supportive pal piped up: "I've had showers that have lasted longer than some of your relationships."

THE YOUNG CHAP in a Glasgow pub was telling his pals that he had split up with his girlfriend because she was psychic. When they asked for an explanation, he told them: "She was seeing people behind my back."

"THE GIRLFRIEND was looking through holiday brochures," said the chap in the Glasgow pub, "so I asked her if she fancied a wee cruise.

"She got very excited until I told her, 'Well, the film star Tom is back on the market according to the newspapers.'"

STILL, there are women who can get their own back. We hear of the Glasgow chap on the train home who phoned his wife and told her: "I'll be home in five minutes. Put the kettle on."

She merely replied: "I don't think the kettle wants to talk to you right now."

A GLASGOW chap in the pub at the weekend was claiming his wife was incredibly jealous as she found a long blonde hair on his jacket and accused him of having an affair.

"That's nothing," said his mate. "My wife found no hair on my jacket – and accused me of cheating on her with a bald woman."

A CHAP in the pub said he couldn't help it when his wife looked up from her magazine and announced: "It says here it would improve your sex life if you just walked 20 minutes a day."

He replied: "Why? Who do I know that lives 20 minutes away?"

A REGULAR in an Ayrshire pub tells us there was surprise when one of the topers announced he was taking his wife to the pictures, as no-one in the pub could recall him ever accompanying his wife on such an occasion. When they asked him what prompted this he replied: "She told me that I took the bins out more often than her. And I couldn't argue with her logic."

STEVEN ELDER writes in: "My wife left a note on the fridge. It said: 'This isn't working anymore. I'm at the end of my tether. I'm away to stay at my mother's.'

"I opened the fridge. The light came on and the beer was cold. Nothing wrong with the fridge. Nae idea what she's on about."

"WHEN I met my girlfriend," said the chap in the Glasgow pub the other day, "she said she loved a man with a sense of humour."

He added: "Now all I get from her is the complaint, 'So is everything just a joke to you?'"

IN Glasgow's west end a newly engaged woman was showing off her diamond solitaire to friends, and announced: "A lot of men are going to be sad when I get married."

"How's that?" asked one of her pals sweetly. "You do know you can only marry one man at a time."

GALES of laughter in a west end bar recently when a group of women were discussing what they had in common with their husbands. One of the ladies was a bit stumped until all she could finally come out with was: "We got married on the same day."

A READER catching a late-night bus in Glasgow heard a young woman angrily tell her boyfriend: "You always blame everyone else when things go wrong."

He savoured the response of the boyfriend: "And whose fault is that?"

HARD to believe there is still the occasional misogynist in Glasgow pubs. One was heard the other night: "I proposed to my ex-wife at the weekend. She said no. Said I was only after her for my money."

ALAN LANG, mine host at Glasgow bar Vroni's, was serving a married couple lunch, and warned them that the pasta was very garlicky "in case you have a wee peck later".

Says Alan: "The husband, quick as a flash, uttered the immortal line, 'That's why I take her everywhere I go – so I don't have to kiss her goodbye.'"

SEEMINGLY women are becoming more impervious to bad chat-up lines. A reader heard one chap in a Glasgow bar avow: "You're the most beautiful woman I have ever seen."

The object of his charm merely replied: "Well I've seen your exes on Facebook, so I believe you."

GLASGOW chat-up lines. A reader says she heard a lad in a city centre bar tell a woman: "I want you to have my children."

She thought that was pretty cringy until he added: "In fact, you can have them right now, they're out in the car."

MONDAY morning, and a lot of folk are on the train going into work in Glasgow. A south side reader hears a chap greet a friend getting on at Muirend and asking him what he did at the weekend.

"Nothing much," he replied. "Shopping."

"What did you buy?" asked the first chap.

"Lorna wanted curtains for the little window in the garage."

The first chap thought about this for some seconds before asking: "Was this before or after she got you a lobotomy?"

A GLASGOW chap tells us he was wondering what the reaction would be when he told his parents he was entering into a civil partnership with his boyfriend.

He reckoned his dad was pretty cool about it as he asked: "Does that mean two stag nights?"

"MY NEW girlfriend could stop traffic," the chap in the Glasgow pub sipping cold lager told his pals at the weekend.

"Bit of a looker is she then?" a drinking buddy piped up.

"Naw, she's a lollipop lady," the chap replied.

A READER tells us he was puzzled when he asked his wife: "What do you fancy this summer, Spain or Portugal?" and she squealed with excitement: "Oh I'd love Portugal."

As he told us: "I was only going to put a pound bet on for her for the Euro championships, so it hardly seemed worthwhile getting that excited."

NEWS from Lanarkshire where Ronnie Buchanan in Larkhall tells us: "Someone knocked on our front door last night and I ignored it, suspecting a cold caller. However it happened a second time and I opened the door to a nice lady who said: 'Hi, I am looking for Love.'

"We looked at each other for what seemed a while. Turned out she was trying to find Mrs Love who stays a few doors down. Had me going for a moment though."

THE chap in the Glasgow pub says he took a brave pill when he arrived home and told his wife: "The house is looking very tidy." He admits he went too far by adding: "Was the internet not working today?"

AH, MARITAL BLISS. Reader Michael Grace heard an old dear in a butcher's shop in Helensburgh complaining about her husband and remarking: "He really annoyed me this morning."

"How's that?" asked the chatty butcher as he prepared her order.

"He got up before I'd left the house," she replied.

KAREN BURKE, manager of Marks Hotel in Glasgow, was recently asked if she ever gets the chance to escape from work.

"Not really," she replied, "My husband's called Mark – and he treats the house like a hotel."

A READER in the west end heard a chap in a trendy pub tell the girl he was talking to that he was going out for a ciggy. "Do you smoke a lot?" she asked him. And the chap, trying to be as positive as he could, replied: "Only when I drink."

It was when she asked him how often he drank that his face clouded over and he answered: "Most days."

4
X Marks The Spot

Politicians take themselves very seriously. Fortunately the voters don't.

WHO could fail to be a fan of Scottish eloquence? Tom Dowds in Cumbernauld tell us: "My daughter was listening to a news item on Spanish television about the local elections in the UK. The only Scot interviewed said he was not going to vote, and when asked why, he replied that the parties 'are two cheeks of the same bum.'"

DURING the Cabinet reshuffle Labour's Jim Murphy, the Eastwood MP, was loving the intrigue. As he put it: "Only one Tory MP at 5-a-side football this morning, the rest at home in the belief that staring at their phone would make it ring."

But perhaps the most colourful reaction was from writer Paul Bassett Davies, not a fan of the Tory Government methinks, who observed: "Expecting us to be excited by this reshuffle is like expecting a corpse to be excited when the gravediggers change shift."

Adventures by Disney - Scotland Vacations

OUR FORMER *Evening Times* colleague, political reporter Ian Hernon, once told us of a Labour conference where the Glasgow trade unionist chairing the session was trying to pick out the next speaker from the delegates holding their hands up. He managed to either horrify or amuse those present by declaring: "That lassie in the red frock. No, not you hen, the pretty one in the next row."

VETERAN politician Tam Dalyell tells in his autobiography, *The Importance of Being Awkward*, that within days of being elected as MP for West Lothian, he mentioned to a local newspaper editor that some Linlithgow residents had complained to him about dog mess in the streets.

The newspaper printed a short story about it, and as soon as the newspaper hit the streets Tam was phoned by the local councillor at eight in the morning. He recalls: "'Tam,' he said, 'Westminster, your business. Dog s***, mine.' Whereupon the telephone was slammed down. That was the first and only occasion I had a brush with West Lothian Council."

ALEX SALMOND had to defend the Scottish education system at First Minister's Questions. A Glasgow reader tells us Mr Salmond's opponents may have a point. Our reader was on a bus into town the other day when a young lad picked up a free newspaper, glanced at a story, then asked his pal: "What kind of animal's a scapegoat?"

TALKING of independence, reader Alex Bowman in Glasgow pleads: "If Scotland ends up breaking away from the UK, can we end up just west of Portugal?"

POLITICS, and Edinburgh Tory councillor Alastair Paisley tells us there is much debate about Scots living in England not being allowed to vote in the independence referendum.

"Someone worked out," he tells us, "that 9 of the 11 players in the Scottish international football team won't be able to vote.

"But not to worry – they're not able to put a cross in the box anyway."

A QUESTION in the Brown Bull pub quiz in Lochwinnoch was: "What did Thomas Sheraton become famous for making?" A team more clued up on famous Scottish perjury trials answered "Mailbags" rather than the "furniture" the quizmaster was actually seeking.

ALLAN MORRISON in King's Park sends us a Theresa May joke.
  "Knock, knock."
  "Come in."

"I SEE on the news," says an observer of the Scottish political scene, "that if you give £250,000 to the Tories you can meet David Cameron.
  "Up here if you give 50 quid to the SNP you can meet Alex Salmond. And for a 100, you don't have to."

THE COUNCIL elections were by the single transferable vote system so voters had to mark ballot papers 1-2-3-4 rather than simply putting an X. We recall the Hibs fan at the last such election who told his pals he had marked his voting slip with the numbers 4- 4-2. When asked why, he replied: "Tactical voting."

VETERAN left-wing campaigner Tony Benn argued at the Edinburgh Book Festival against hereditary peers sitting in the House of Lords. As Tony put it: "I wouldn't be impressed if I went to a dentist and he said to me: 'I'm not a dentist myself, but my father was a rather good one.'"

IT'S A SHAME our voting booths don't have curtains like they do in some American states. We remember one American comic who claimed his voting tradition was "Enter booth. Pull curtain. Remove trousers. Wait 10 seconds. Then lean out and say, 'Do you have these in a 34?'"

AFTER *Britain's Got Talent's* final on the telly, a reader writes: "I'm losing faith in the British public and their right to vote. First Cameron, and now a dancing dog."

GREAT NEWS that former Dunfermline footballer and manager Jim Leishman has become Provost of Fife. We remember Jim telling a fundraising dinner in Glasgow that as a young player he could have signed for Liverpool, Manchester United, or Chelsea.

"But none of them wanted me," he added, "so I signed for Dunfermline."

KENNY KEMP was in Edinburgh's Waverley Station when he overheard a traveller tell a companion: "Did you know my granny's died?"

"No, I'm so sorry to hear that, how old was she?" replied his concerned friend.

"No. Magranny, the Lockerbie bombing guy."

MICHAEL GOVE, David Cameron's Education Secretary, may seem the epitome of a Home Counties Tory, but he was brought up in Aberdeen.

That would probably explain why, according to leading political information service, Dods, he told a lobby lunch – that's a lunch with journalists, not one that's a sit-doon in the hall – that "Rangers has a new buyer: a German millionaire living in Italy.

"It turned out to be the Pope."

THE SCOTTISH Government's wish to lower the age for voting in the future referendum to 16, makes Martin Morrison in Lochinver suggest that if that happens then an additional answer should be added to the ballot paper. The three answers should then be Yes, No, or Whatever.

AND OUR MENTION of 16-year-olds possibly voting in the independence referendum leads to David Kelso suggesting that simply ticking a box will no longer be enough. "These young voters," says David, "will want to write beside the various options 'OMG!' or 'LOL.'"

THE BUDGET was being widely discussed when a reader was asked by a colleague at work: "If the economy's slowing down, how come it's so hard for me to keep up with it?"

5
Out Of The Mouths Of Babes

A READER in Glasgow tells us an office colleague announced the other day: "I have a cold shower every morning."

Everyone was thinking how hardy that must be when the chap added: "Right after my wife and daughters have finally finished having hot ones."

DADS who think they're funny. A young Lanarkshire girl was keen to have some pet goldfish, so while searching the cupboard she shouted out: "Have you seen the fish bowl?"

"No," shouted back Dad, "but I think I saw the cat playing darts once."

WE sometimes think you have to be bilingual in Lanarkshire. A reader tells us that her Lanarkshire niece came home from her dancing classes with awards in tap, majorette and cheerleading. Gazing at her various rosettes and certificates, the young one asked her dad: "What does certificate of merit mean?" Before he had a chance to answer she added: "Oh, silly me, that's when you're married, isn't it?"

AH the generation gap. A Milngavie reader realised her grandson had never seen loose tea leaves because the family always used tea bags. "Fortune tellers used to read tea leaves," she told him in a bout of reminiscing.

"I didn't even know you could write on them," he told her.

AN ABERDEENSHIRE reader was visiting his 10-year-old granddaughter who was excitedly telling him about her cheerleading course, and reading from the leaflet about what they were being taught. She explained she could do a backward roll, a handstand and a back flip. Reading further, she announced: "And I can do an ektektekt!" Not knowing this particular feat of gymnastics, he took the leaflet and read at the end of the list "Etc, etc, etc."

A SUPPLY teacher tells us he is covering for a teacher who has gone off to have a baby. A first-year pupil asked him: "Is she on eternity leave?" His reply of: "She probably wishes she was," perhaps went over her head.

OUT of the mouths of babes . . . Jim McGinlay in Gardgate tells us his daughter was driving her three tired children home, but didn't want them falling asleep in the car.

Seeing her two-year-old with her eyes closed, she told her: "Don't you close your eyes!"

"I'm not", came the reply, "I'm just looking at my eyelids."

IT'S STILL a daily task to dodge the folk trying to sign you up for charities as they prowl the pedestrian precinct near the Concert Hall in Glasgow. A reader tells us about one such worker who threw her arms wide and asked a passing father with his small boy if he would "like to save a child today".

He merely pointed to his son and told her: "You can start wi' him. Good luck hen!" and carried on walking.

DADS who think they are funny, continued. A south side girl wishing to sprinkle cheese on her spaghetti asked: "Where's the cheese grater?"

"Some would say France, others would say Cheddar in England," dad replied from the dinner table.

A PRIMARY teacher tells us he is concerned about how much television features in the lives of his little charges. He claimed he asked one pupil: "What's 41 and 70?" The tot replied: "Sky Sports and CBBC channels."

A TEACHER tells us she is desperate for the summer holidays after stopping two lads jostling in the school corridors whom she didn't recognise and asking them: "What year are you in?" The braver of the two replied: "2012."

A LENZIE reader tells us he felt old when he tried to explain to his teenage daughter that in his day there were no comprehensive schools and you had to sit the 11-Plus to decide what school you went to. "Eleven plus what?" asked his daughter.

DISAPPEARING guid Scots words continued. Matt Vallance recalls: "There was a guy a couple of years below me at Cumnock Academy, Hugh Middleditch, whose nickname was that fine word Sheugh."

ANGELA SIMMS tells us about picking up her seven-year-old granddaughter from school, and the conversation turning to a family wedding they had all recently attended.

"Why?" asked the little one with some puzzlement, "did the minister ask if the groom would take her to be his awful wedded wife?"

A BEARSDEN dad says his son came rushing in from the kitchen and declared: "I just melted an ice cube by staring at it."

He then added: "Took a bit longer than I thought it would, though."

DAFT GAG from the playground. "I know my goldfish loves it when I take him out of his bowl.

"He wags his tail a lot."

A SCOUT leader in the suburbs of Edinburgh was lost for words after he had set the lads the task of monitoring what birds visited their gardens over recent days. One chap said he had seen either a cormorant or a shag in his garden. But another nine-year-old, who knew that such sea birds rarely travelled so far inland, shouted out: "You can't get a shag in Balerno!"

OUR STORY about bird identification in the garden reminds retired teacher Margaret Thomson in Kilmacolm: "I took my class to the park to look for birds. A wee lad yelled out, 'Hey Miss, here's a burd. It's eating a biscuit!' I rushed over, bird book in hand, What kind is it? Came the reply, 'Don't know, Miss. Ah think it's a digestive!'"

BIRD identification continued. "When I was teaching in Drumchapel," says reader Bob Byiers, "a seagull landed outside our classroom window, and we were all alerted by a budding ornithologist exclaiming, 'Sur, err a eagle on ra windae sill an' it's staunin' oan wan paw!' And there was I trying to teach said ornithologist to speak French."

A READER who bumped into a pal who has two sons congratulated him on the news that his wife was pregnant with their third child.

"Thank you," said the prospective father. "If it's a girl we're going to call her Isabella. If it's a boy we're going to call it quits."

WE HEAR about a schoolgirl in Glasgow's west end who didn't believe her mother when she told her the school was having a dress down day on Friday and that she didn't need to wear her uniform. She came home in a huff as she had been the only person in uniform that day, and blamed her mother.

"How's it my fault?" asked her bemused mum.

"You didn't argue with me long enough," replied the girl.

6
I'll Drink To That

Pubs are closing down at a fast rate in Scotland as more folk drink at home. It's a pity as you would miss conversations like these.

A GLASGOW chap arrived in his local, took out his smart-phone and showed his pals a photo of his new girlfriend while observing: "She's beautiful isn't she?"

"If you think she's gorgeous, you should see my girlfriend," replied one of the chaps.

"Why? Is she a stunner?" he replied. "No, she's an optician," came the droll reply.

A READER was in a city centre pub toilet where a member of staff had put a little typed notice on the cubicle door stating: "Handel broke." Their wayward spelling had allowed someone to write neatly below it: "Beethoven a bit strapped for cash too."

LUNCHTIME drinking is of course a thing of the past for most workers these days.

One retired boss in Glasgow tells us a few of his younger staff were drinking vodka at lunchtime so that their breath wouldn't smell of alcohol.

He told them that he would prefer if they drank whisky as he thought it would be better if the customers thought they were drunk rather than just stupid.

A GROUP of young lads in a Glasgow pub were discussing a mutual friend who they all agreed was a bit slow on the uptake. Eventually one of them declared: "I was with him in a club when this young woman asked him to show her a good time.

"So he took out his holiday snaps from Ibiza."

A TOPER in a Glasgow bar the other night, on being asked about his weekend, replied that he had suffered "classic withdrawal symptoms."

Asked for further enlightenment, he replied: "My head was sore, my bank account had been emptied out and I had three ATM receipts in my pocket."

LOTHIAN ladies Kate McGregor and Linda Tweedie have just published their book *Life Behind Bars: Confessions of a Pub Landlady*. We are much taken with their description of pub quiz teams. They state: "The average pub quiz is not taken seriously, except for the Quizzers.

"These are teams of intellectuals who never miss a match and are normally sourced from the social work department or the local primary school. Their teams have Latin names that not even they can pronounce, and they consume half a lager and a packet of crisps between them, that is until they win first prize when it's brandy and coke all round."

"MY DOC says I've to take up a hobby that gets me out of the pub," said the toper in the pub the other night.

"So I've taken up smoking," he added.

A YOUNG reader tells of being asked for identification at a Glasgow club to prove he was legally entitled to sup alcohol. Behind him, a more senior gentleman, with a girl half his age on his arm, tried to joke with the doorman: "Why don't you ask for my ID?"

Full marks, says our reader, to the steward for replying: "Bus passes don't count."

A READER having a quiet pint in Glasgow's Sloan's Bar before heading home after work, was shocked by, but also a little bit in awe of, the chap sitting further along the horseshoe bar who answered his phone, out of which a female voice could be heard asking him where he was.

The chap had the nerve to reply: "Do you remember when we were walking through the Argyll Arcade and we stopped to admire a diamond eternity ring in the jeweller's window, but we thought it was too expensive?" Then added after a pause: "Well I'm in the pub opposite it."

AH, the dangers of trying to be funny on Twitter. Alan Crossan at Glasgow's revered Clutha Bar decided to promote their new bistro

by posting tongue-in-cheek tweets with the latest being "Annual Kamikaze Pilots reunion dinner tonight at 8pm".

Says Alan: "Unfortunately our young waitresses saw this as an opportunity to meet a pilot. Considering the extra time they spent in front of the mirror we didn't have the heart to tell them. Our general manager Saverio told the disappointed girls that the pilots had cancelled due to the bad weather."

"WHEN ONE door closes, another one opens," said the chap in the Glasgow pub the other night.

"That's why I won't hire that carpenter again."

OVERHEARD in a Glasgow pub the other night: "The doctor looked me squarely in the eye, and said I should give up drinking immediately as it was doing untold damage to my liver.

"So I told him, 'You always say that when it's your round. Get the beers in, you skinflint.'"

WE ASSUME the chap in the Glasgow pub at the weekend was joking when he was asked how his baby was getting on, and he mused: "The wife always thinks it's cute when the baby throws up on me.

"But when it's the other way around, she gets all huffy and accuses me of being drunk."

AS WINE sales rocket in bars, Alan Lang at Vroni's in Glasgow recalls a simpler time when he managed another city wine bar some years ago and a chap ordered for his female companion 'a Glaswegian wine'. Says Alan: "Eventually, having asked him three times and three times his girlfriend whispering her order to him, which he now snarled at me with a fixed stare, did I break the rules and ask her directly. To which she replied: 'A glass of medium white wine.'"

"MY MATE does a brilliant bird impression," said the chap in the pub the other night.

"He takes three hours to get ready for a night out."

"I'VE BEEN on the go since first thing this morning," said the chap meeting his mates in a Glasgow pub. He added: "I really am a terrible *Monopoly* player."

IT SEEMS chaps in pubs can't stop themselves from telling bad jokes. A reader was in his local in Paisley at the weekend when a regular announced: "Did you hear that Alex fell into the upholstery machine at the Reid's factory?" "How is he?" asked a shocked, but gullible, mate.

"He's fully recovered," the first chap triumphantly answered.

PHILOSOPHICAL point raised in a Glasgow pub this week by a regular: "Why do people never admit to being just the right amount of whelmed?"

DOUGIE McNICOL in Bridge of Weir attests to the growing popularity of wine among bar patrons. A new member of staff at his local was restocking the bar's wine rack when she suddenly called to the manager: "This stuff's out of date."

She then showed the puzzled manager the label: "Below where it says pinot grigio, it says 2010."

A TERRIBLE thing the drink. A Glasgow reader was in a city bar beside two chaps who had clearly been on the sauce most of the day. One of them nudged his pal, pointed across the bar, and told him: "Look at the state of them. That'll be us in ten years."

"That's a mirror ya eedjit," his pal replied.

A READER having a beer in the west end was impressed by the comeback when one pretentious chap declared to those around him: "I don't ever watch television."

He was trumped by another chap putting on a puzzled face and asking: "What's television?"

A DIARY fan in Partick spots in a newspaper the claim that "Sixteen-year-olds are drinking twice as much as they did 10 years ago" and he thinks to himself: "Well they would do – they were only six then."

7
All Of A Twitter

Technology and social media is transforming our lives. Not everyone though is happy at the pace of it.

WE HEAR of the computer repair shop in Glasgow that had difficulty with its support staff phoning customers to offer them a software update.

It seems that phoning folk and saying: "Ahm gonnae come roon and put your Windows in," wasn't regarded as all that welcoming.

LIVELY PLACE Glasgow on a Saturday night. A reader in the Central Station taxi queue heard a short-skirted young lady slur at her pal: "Did you see that Sophie had slagged you aff oan Facebook?" "Aye," replied her pal. "Mair like Two-face Book."

TECHNOLOGY is changing our lives in more ways than we realise. A Gourock reader tells us: "My wife received a text message from my seven-year-old son while she was doing the dishes last night.

"It said: 'Finished. Come and wipe my bottom.' So she did."

INTERNET security is, of course, a growing problem, and almost daily computer users are sent warnings to avoid viruses in attachments that could harm their computers.

We received an e-mail which stated: "Warning. If you receive a message saying you have won two free tickets to see Rangers at Ibrox, DO NOT OPEN. You have actually won two tickets to see Rangers at Ibrox."

TALKING of technology, Mike Ritchie on Glasgow's south side tells us: "A female chum leaving a wine bar after lunch realised when outside she had left her trendy black beret inside. Back inside, she explained to the waiter she needed to look for it to see if it was under a chair or a table. 'Why don't we just ring the number and we'll find it that way?' he said, helpfully."

"SOMETIMES I think the only reason I have a home phone," we overhear a woman in Byres Road chatting to her friend, "is to use it to find my mobile phone in the house."

A STIRLINGSHIRE reader fulminates: "Sadly I fear it's only a matter of time before the wedding vows in church end with the minister saying: 'I now pronounce you husband and wife.

"'You may now update your Facebook status.'"

THE POPULAR online encyclopaedia *Wikipedia* closed down for a day to protest against new laws in America.

"It will be interesting to see tomorrow's homework," a Glasgow secondary school teacher told us.

THE ROYAL BANK'S decision to sack Scottish workers and move jobs to India reminds Ian MacLean of when he worked at Lloyds TSB and a customer phoned the bank's call centre in India to say she had lost her husband, and needed information about their joint account.

The polite call-centre worker dutifully answered her query, and earnestly ended the call by hoping that she would find her husband soon.

SAYS DOUGIE McNICOL: "A friend on a visit to his son and daughter-in-law asked if they had a newspaper. "Dad," scoffed the son, "this is the 21st century. We don't do newspapers. Use my iPad."

"Say what you like about new technology," the friend later told Dougie. "That fly never knew what hit it!"

DATING it seems is still a complicated business. A reader in a Byres Road pub heard a young student-type tell his pal that he had split up with his girlfriend. The chap then added: "The day after she dumped me she phoned to ask how you change your relationship status on Facebook."

JIM FITZPATRICK tells us about a friend renewing her car insurance by telephone.

Says Jim: "The Q&A session was going well until she was asked if she was hormonal. At this point she lost the plot and had a bit of a rant at the telesales person over this stupid and blatantly sexist question. When he eventually managed to calm her down he said, 'I am sorry madam but you must have misheard me. I asked you if you were a homeowner.'"

CALL CENTRES again, and a reader tells us: "My call was answered by someone who said they would transfer me to a 'specialist'. Sadly I didn't realise their speciality was playing Vivaldi for 20 minutes before I hung up."

OUR STORIES of misunderstandings by call centre staff remind David Martin: "I remember ordering books by telephone, and the person on the other end asked, 'How do you spell Menzieshill?' I replied, 'Exactly as you say it.'

"I guess it was lost on someone without a Scottish tongue."

AN EDINBURGH reader tells us he took his mum out for Sunday lunch where she looked across at another table before telling him: "Isn't it lovely to see people praying before their food arrives?" He didn't have the heart to tell her that the couple were both looking down at their smart phones while texting.

THE NEWS that the Government-owned Royal Bank of Scotland is to sack workers in Scotland and transfer their jobs to India reminds Fraser Kelly in Singapore of the classic yarn of the Kelvinside lady who tries to phone her local bank branch but is put through to an Indian call centre. She insists: "I want to talk to Mary in my local branch," but the chap who answered doggedly tells her: "Madam, I have two degrees, and have been superbly trained by the RBS. I can do anything for you that this Mary can."

"I don't think so," she tells him. But he stands his ground: "Madam, I have the finest IT system here and can tell you anything faster than any branch person in Scotland can."

"Ok," she finally relents. "Did I leave my gloves on the branch counter this morning?"

THERE'S BEEN a huge rise, of course, in goods being ordered online for home delivery but it can lead to frustrations.

As a reader waiting at home all day phoned to ask us: "Do you think if you go for a job interview to become an Argos delivery driver, they are ok with it if you say you'll turn up for the interview anytime between 7am and 7pm?"

OUR STORY of Facebook mis-spellings reminds a reader of having to keep his face straight when his daughter posted on Facebook "I love the smell of Paul's colon."

He is really hoping it is a reference to after-shave rather than a deep interest in anatomy.

"I DON'T like to think," declared a student on Byres Road, "about all the time I've wasted on Twitter which I could have spent watching television."

DAFT technology gag. A man tells his doctor: "You have to help me. I'm addicted to Twitter." Replies the doc: "Sorry, I don't follow you."

A READER tells us about a fellow mother at the school gate who shook her head and declared: "My daughter's 11, and has an iPhone. When I was 11, I was happy with a Cabbage Patch doll."

READER Ronnie Dillin in East Kilbride had to spell his name out phonetically to a travel firm's call centre worker as his surname is frequently spelled as Dillon unless he is quite specific. So he told her: "R Dillin. Romeo, Delta, India, Lima, Lima, India, November."

He thought he had done rather well until the woman replied: "I've never spoken to someone called Romeo before."

A RUMOUR spread across Twitter that veteran Radio Clyde DJ Tiger Tim Stevens had died. He hadn't.

Curiously, in life imitating art, or something like that, Tiger lost his job as Celtic Park DJ when he announced before a European tie that there would be a minute's silence. As the crowd wondered whether a former player or director had snuffed it, Tim added: "In memory of Rangers' European Cup campaign, which was declared dead earlier today in Bulgaria" a reference to city rivals Rangers going out earlier that day to a last-minute goal.

Everyone laughed – apart from the directors it seems, as Tim was never asked back for microphone duties.

AS YOUNGSTERS expect more and more complex smart-phones as Christmas presents, a Troon reader is reminded of when mobile phones first appeared, and were the size and weight of a substantial house brick. He was walking down the road at lunchtime back then with a smug colleague who had such a phone in his briefcase.

When he heard a beeping noise the smug colleague announced that was his mobile phone ringing. But as he delved in his case our reader was able to tell him: "Sorry, it's actually the pedestrian crossing we've just passed."

AN UDDINGSTON reader tells us that not every call centre worker is really thinking very well when they are at work. He had to phone a company he had previously ordered goods from and the person on the phone said they just had to check that his details hadn't changed. "Is your address still the same?" he asked. Then: "Phone number?" And finally: "Date of birth?"

EARLY mobile phones continued. Mary Bunting in Ayrshire was lecturing at Kilmarnock College when she placed her brick-sized mobile phone on her desk. An admiring female student told her that if ever she was attacked, she could clobber her assailant with the phone, then phone for the polis with the same implement.

Yes you couldn't do that with a smart phone.

A READER tells us one of the rules of Facebook. She explains: "You know you are losing an argument on Facebook when you are reduced to correcting the other person's grammar."

OUR TALE of the girl on Facebook who admired the smell of a boy's 'colon' brings forth from a reader: "Being a geriatric divorcée, I joined an internet dating website. I live in England where it's very obvious that most of the ladies on the database did not have the benefit of a 'good Scottish education'. There are some interesting spelling mistakes, spoonerisms and malapropisms, but the best, so far, is a lady whose profile name is 'Sweatlips.'"

8
Face-lifts And Coffee

A CLARKSTON reader at Glasgow's Central Station watched a young gum-chewing woman with her dyed blonde hair harshly scraped back from her face and tied in a bun, walk past two chaps who eyed her up.

After she had passed, one of them told his mate: "That's what they call a Castlemilk face-lift."

A READER out and about in the west end watched as a lothario at the bar offered to buy some middle-aged woman on a night out some champagne.

"Oh I had a bad experience with champagne once," replied one of the ladies.

"We had it at my wedding."

A PARTICK reader overhears a couple of students discussing their girlfriends in the pub. One of them declared: "The fuse went in the flat the other night, plunging us into darkness. I was trying to fix it when the girlfriend piped up, 'Will the toilet still flush?'"

A JORDANHILL mother confesses to us that she came off her new exercise bike at home sweating profusely, only for her puzzled young daughter to ask: "Is that your fat crying?"

A READER phones to tell us: "I told a woman at work that her eyebrows were drawn on too low."

He added: "She looked furious."

A YOUNG woman being chatted up in Glasgow's west end later described the chap to her pals as a "Rangers". When they asked for clarification, she explained: "Not in my league."

A WEST End reader overhears a Sauvignon-swilling woman in an Ashton Lane bar musing on the passage of time. "You know you're getting old," she told the folk with her, "when your friends start having kids on purpose.

FRIENDS, of course, are not always the most supportive of people. A reader in a Glasgow nightclub heard a young woman moan to her pal: "I wish someone would like me for my brain."

"What about a zombie then?" replied her less-than-caring companion.

"MY wife always likes to put on a happy face," said the chap in the pub the other night.

"Which might explain why she got sacked from the make-up counter at a department store."

A READER hears some women in a Glasgow coffee shop discussing a mutual friend who is thinking of having surgery to help reduce her weight.

"So she's jumping on the gastric band wagon?" one of them asked.

A READER tells us he was building some flat-packed furniture for his daughter while being watched by his eagle-eyed grandchild. As the flimsy tools that came with it proved useless, he asked the young boy if he knew where a screwdriver was. "I'll get you mummy's screwdriver!" the little one shouted, and disappeared.

He came back two minutes later with a side-plate cutlery knife.

WE had better not name the reader who told us: "The number plate was missing from the front of my car so I went to the garage and got a new one.

"My wife was amazed they had one in stock, with our number."

OVERHEARD in a Motherwell pub the other day: "When the doorbell rings at home the dog always runs to it, and the wife said to me, 'Why does he always think it's for him?'"

A TYRE fitter on Glasgow's south side was dealing with a customer who was complaining that her front tyres seemed to wear down awfully quickly, so he suggested that in future she rotate them to lengthen their life.

The puzzled woman asked him: "But don't they rotate automatically as I'm driving?"

A READER on the Edinburgh to Glasgow train noted three raucous women on board, encumbered with shopping after, presumably, a day of retail and pinot grigio therapy. Across from them a fellow traveller's phone rang and he was heard telling the caller that yes, he knew he should have been home by then but he had to work late at the office, and no, he had not gone for a drink after work, and no, he had not gone for a drink with the new receptionist.

The demeanour of the chap on the phone, says our reader, was not helped by one of the ladies opposite, when he denied having a drink with the receptionist, shouting across: "Put that phone down and come back to bed."

A CHAP in the pub the other night was telling his pals that he had been quite nervous on a recent flight when he discovered that the pilot was female.

"Oh that's so sexist of you," one of his mates replied. "It's not as if she had to reverse it."

A READER tells us he had just returned from a two-day conference when his wife told him: "I've got a surprise for you in the bedroom."

Sadly his hopes were cruelly dashed when she added: "I've put the winter quilt on."

WEST END bar conversations are often fascinating. A young woman arrived back from the crowded bar on Friday night and told her pals at the table: "Would you believe that the guy at the bar managed to guess my star sign was Cancer straight away!" Her more cynical pal replied: "I take it you had already told him your name was June."

"Why?" replied her baffled pal.

AH THE UNIVERSAL problem of fathers having to cope with what their teenage daughters wear on a night out. One Giffnock father admits that when his daughter came downstairs recently he couldn't stop himself asking: "Are you a vampire?" When the puzzled girl answered in the negative, he added: "I just assumed you couldn't see your reflection in a mirror."

WHO SAYS Wishaw doesn't move with the times? David Stevenson was visiting the Lanarkshire town where he tried out a branch of the coffee chain Costa. Says David: "Contemplating one of the coffee purveyor's posters on the wall which claimed that their 'Coffee is made with amore', the wee wumman at the next table, clearly puzzled, jabbed her hapless man in the ribs and demanded, 'John, made with mair whit?'"

A QUEUE formed at coffee shop Starbucks at Glasgow's Queen Street station when the company held their giveaway promotion "A free latte with your name on it". Reader Frank Murphy reports: "The queue cracked up when the barista holding a felt tip pen to write on the cup asked their next customer: 'What's your name?'

"Shouting from further back in the queue was a fan of *Dad's Army* who declared: 'Don't tell him, Pike!'"

A KELVINSIDE reader tells us that when he flipped open his wallet in a west end cafe, his bright blue and red donor card was very prominent, and the chatty waitress asked if he was an organ donor.

He is still puzzled by the fact that after he said yes, she asked: "Did it hurt?"

FANCY COFFEE continued. Andy Cumming tells us he was in Starbucks in Glasgow and noticed a big lipstick stain on the mug after he took his first sip. Says Andy: "I marched up to the top of the queue to remonstrate with the barista. As the words came out my mouth about their mug hygiene, I recognise the shade as my wife's whom I had kissed goodbye outside only two minutes earlier.

"I slinked off saying to the amusement to the queue of regulars, 'It's OK, it's my own.'"

AN EDINBURGH reader noticed a city chip shop that had to display a notice in its window from health inspectors detailing an infestation of mice discovered on the premises. No doubt the notice was ordered by health inspectors as a deterrent. But our reader wonders how effective it was.

Someone else had taped a notice to the outside of the window on which they had written: "Who cares about mice? I dinnae go tae a chippy tae get healthy."

A GLASGOW reader wonders how many waiters in the city think they are comedians.

In an amiable fashion the other night, he said to his server: "It looks like rain," and the chap just had to reply: "I know, but that's how the soup comes in here."

```
sweets
  Chocolate Fudge Cake                    3.25
  Sticky Toffee Pudding                   3.25
  Daily Grumble                           3.25
  Ice Cream                               1.95

ft tea/coffee
  Teas                                    1.50
  Latte (for god's sake get a grip)      11.95
  Coffee Black or White                   1.95
  Cappuccino                              2.00
  Espresso                                1.60

The Griffin Bar   266 Bath St   Glasgow   G2 4JP   0141 331 5
```

DOUGLAS KINNAIRD from Glasgow had taken his wife to Edinburgh where they stopped in a bar for a drink. "What's the prosecco like?" Mrs K asked the waiter, thinking she might try the sparkling wine.

After some hesitation, the waiter replied: "I don't know. I was on a training day when they explained all the wines, but I drank so much I don't remember anything."

MUSICIAN Bruce MacGregor of the band Blazin' Fiddles mentioned on Facebook that he had a couple of unsatisfactory meals on his last visit to Edinburgh.

A fan replied that a local worthy in Edinburgh once found a dead seagull, went into his local takeaway, slammed it on the counter and said: "That's the last one I supply till you've paid for the rest."

There was then a sudden exit by everyone waiting for food.

FORMER Central Hotel page boy Desmond Lynn tells in the sumptuous history of the hotel, *Glasgow's Grand Central Hotel* by Bill Hicks and Jill Scott, of comedy duo Laurel and Hardy staying there and waving to the thousands of fans thronging Hope Street.

Oliver Hardy asked for a pen or pencil to sign autographs, and Desmond handed him his pencil. When Oliver remarked on how small the pencil was, Desmond boldly replied: "Not as small as your sixpenny tip."

The duo laughed, took the hint, and handed Desmond a princely five shillings each.

THE BOOK also tells of the fine dining at the Central where a guest at a dinner to mark the launch of a ship at the Fairfield yard asked a waiter how to eat the asparagus tips with butter he had just been served.

"Just hang back and watch another table," replied the waiter.

NOT EVERYONE in Dundee is very worldly it seems. Scott Barclay was in a kebab shop late on Friday night in the city when a chap being served in front of him leaned over the counter and announced: "A wid like bacon oan mine."

Says Scott: "The reply from across the salad bar was, 'I'm sorry, we're halal'.

"Once again the man lurched onto the counter with a smile glazed on his face. However this time he presented his hand and politely responded, 'Oh, awright Halal, Ma name's Sam.'"

9
Wearing A Boiler Suit

A MEMORIAL concert was held to mark the 40th anniversary of the UCS work-in that saved the Clyde shipyards. It reminds us of the story told against Jimmy Airlie and Jimmy Reid, the charismatic leaders of the work-in.

As Donald Macaskill tells us: "Jimmy Reid and Jimmy Airlie were standing in the canteen queue when Airlie fell to the floor in a dead faint.

"A puzzled Jimmy Reid said, 'I just asked if I could get him a bowl of soup.' Airlie, now in the recovery position, gasped, 'God, I thought you said boiler suit.'"

AS WE WERE reminiscing about the shipyards, Russell Martin in Bearsden tells us: "The yard manager is doing his daily rounds of the shipyard when he sees a man being carried down the gangway of a ship on a stretcher. He asks a passing workman if there has been an accident.

"'Naw', came the reply, 'They're jist moving a welder to a joab on anither boat.'"

WE ASKED for tales from the shipyards, and Jim Morrison tells us: "A cousin of mine was once a boilermaker in Kvaerner shipyard in sunny Govan. One day he and his foreman were walking across the yard when they were accosted by a large Norwegian manager, who asked them, 'Can't you walk any faster?'

"'Look pal, this is a biler suit am wearing – no a track suit,' replied the foreman."

ENTERTAINER Andy Cameron recalls: "The tales reminded me of one of the old shipyard characters of which every yard on the Clyde had one.

"Jimmy McCrindle, aka The Pig, was a legend in Govan.

"The gaffer was passing him one day and enquired, 'Is that whisky Ah can smell off your breath McCrindle?'

"The Pig replies, 'It better be or that licenced grocer on Govan Road is gettin' a doin.'"

A FORMER shop steward in the yards tells us how union recruitment was carried out. "I'd approach each new recruit on their first day and ask if they were in the union. If they said 'no', I just telt them, 'Well, ye ur noo!'"

IT WAS a mainly mature audience at the UCS work-in anniversary concert at Glasgow's Old Fruitmarket.

As veteran performer Jimmie Macgregor told the audience: "Ronnie

Scott of Ronnie Scott's jazz club once said that you can look young by associating with old people. So thanks very much for coming along tonight."

SHIPYARD TALES remind us of the pay negotiations at the old John Brown's yard where a shop steward declared: "Ah've tellt ye . . . nae mair moolah, the bears are oot!" An American executive turned to a local colleague for elucidation, only to be told: "Basically, he's sayin' the ba's on the slates."

OUR UNION meeting story reminds Bill McLean in Johnstone, clearly a movie fan: "I went to a union meeting in the 1970s where I asked a pal what he thought the outcome would be. 'It will be Quo Vadis as usual,' he replied.

"I asked if he meant 'status quo' rather than 'quo vadis', but he said he meant quo vadis because we will be thrown to the lions again."

JIM McDONALD in Carluke reminds us of being an apprentice in Fairfield's in the 60s when he was told there was a journeymen v apprentices road race between Govan Cross and Shieldhall, with the journeymen being given three yards of a start because of the age difference.

The wind-up continued until the penny dropped that the three yards of a start were Harland and Wolf, Fairfield's and Alexander Stephens.

JOE O'ROURKE in Port Glasgow recalls: "I was a shop steward in Scott Lithgow's Kingston yard when the company decided to step up security because of thefts.

"So one Monday several guys built like all-in wrestlers appeared in the yard; all walking around with their chests stuck out, looking very menacing indeed. Well that was until they went for their tea-break at 10 o'clock; someone had stolen the electric kettle out of their office."

JOE ALSO remembers: "As a shop steward I was sent for by the manager with one of the caulker burners. When we entered the office the manager had all these papers on his desk, he said, 'Danny, that's your timekeeping record for the last two years. In that time you've only worked one Monday. How do you explain that?' 'I must have been skint that Monday,' said Danny."

WE ASKED for your shipyard stories, and Hugh Campbell tells us: "A foreman checking the work of a pipefitter was heard to comment, 'Cry yersel' a fitter son? Ye couldny fit a nut in a monkey's mooth!'"

MOVING on from the nicknames of shipyard workers, Craig Crawford in Howwood says: "A taxi driver once assured me there was a certain taxi driver who worked at Glasgow Airport who would have his taxi meter switched on before a client got in, so increasing the fare – he was nicknamed President Mitterand."

THE REV. JOHN GILLIES in Dailly, Ayrshire, remembers an organist at another church who referred to his wife as his 'melancholy baby'. When John asked why he had given her the unusual nickname he replied: "Oh she's got a heid like a melon, and a face like a collie."

BEING a delivery driver must be one of the more stressful jobs in the run-up to Christmas. We hear of one depot in Lanarkshire where a tardy driver is nicknamed The Wife. It's because his fellow drivers claim he always takes things the wrong way.

EDINBURGH SNP councillor Stefan Tymkewycz tells us that when he was in the police there was a workshy officer who never took any prisoners. He was known as Gurkha.

A RENFREWSHIRE secondary teacher tells us: "One of our janitors was a very small, jolly and rather rotund man. He was known to the senior pupils as 'Jannie DeVito.'"

NICKNAMES, and Peter Wright tells us of a joiner called 'lightning' because he could never hit the same place twice.

WE LIKED Bill Wilson's anecdote in *Off the Run*, the magazine of Strathclyde Fire & Rescue Retired Employees Association.

One day, on a full turn-out from Glasgow's South Fire Station, the three engines arrived at a road junction. The first turned right, the second turned left and the third, unsure which way to go, decided to shoot straight ahead.

It was because of this that the South station watch became known within the service as the Red Arrows.

JIM COOK in Airdrie recalls the clerk of works on one building site who was never satisfied with the work of the painters, and would point at a finished wall and shout: "Repaint!" He was known as The Evangelist.

JOHN LAWSON recounts: "A former colleague, who had a deplorable attendance record, was known as The Madonna – she made rare appearances, and when she did, it was a miracle."

DOUGAL McLAUCHLAN says there used to be a police superintendent known by his colleagues as Semmit because he was never off their backs. Hugh Gillies says: "An office inspector at Clydebank cop shop was known as The Snowman – any time he was asked to do anything, the reply was, 'S'no ma job.'"

NICKNAMES continued. Says Robert McMillar: "In the factory where I worked, in Paisley, there was a supervisor whose nickname was Subway – this being due to the fact that he came round every ten minutes, to check up that you were working."

ALISTAIR THOMSON, now in Canada, recalls the St Patrick's High School teacher in Dumbarton whose surname was McCollum, a less common spelling of McCallum, which is often found in Ireland. The pupils immediately nicknamed him "Widgy".

10
Having Your Day In Court

GLASGOW Sheriff Court is of course still one of the busiest courts in Europe. A Newlands reader who arrived for jury duty wondered how fair the jury was going to be when one of his fellow jurists confided: "When the letter arrived with the court address on the envelope, I thought it was a summons."

IT'S TOUGH being a lawyer these days. A Glasgow reader tells us his lawyer friend was bemoaning the fact the downturn in the housing market had affected the once lucrative conveyancing business, and that much of his turnover was now coming from dealing with wills and estates. "Mind you," he added, "this mild winter hasn't helped much either."

THE NEW Low Moss prison opened near Bishopbriggs, catering for 700 prisoners. A local swears to us that a bouncer from a Glasgow nightclub wanted more job security and applied to be a prison officer there. He failed the interview, alas, when he was asked: "There will be some tough individuals here. How would you handle it if trouble broke out?"

"No problem," he replied. "I'd just tell them if they didn't behave then they'd be straight out the door."

WE BLAME all these dodgy daytime television advertisements, but a police officer swears to us he attended a road traffic accident where the driver was still in his vehicle. "Are you seriously hurt?" the police officer asked him.

"How would I know," the driver replied. "I'm not a lawyer."

OUR TALES of courts dealing with drunken offenders reminds retired police officer Colin Simpson of the inspector at Glasgow's Govan police office who, when drunks kept in the cell overnight were brought before him to be bailed in the morning, would simply ask them in mock surprise: "How did you end up in Rothesay?" before sending the worried lags out into the streets of Govan.

TONY SYKES in Glasgow was in court when a young man who had been charged with being drunk and incapable in the nurses' hostel at the local hospital asked if he could call the nurses as witnesses to confirm he had not been incapable as "Ah've ma' reputation to think of," as he explained.

A GLASGOW lawyer swears on oath to us that a recidivist appearing at a Justice of the Peace Court for some drink-related crime was told by the exasperated JP that the accused had been appearing before him for the past ten years.

The accused merely replied: "It's not my fault you can't get promoted."

A CHAP in the pub was explaining that when he was stopped for speeding he told the traffic cop that he was simply trying to keep up with the traffic.

"There is no traffic," the officer told him.

"That's how far behind I am," the chap argued.

A GLASGOW lawyer tells us he had an elderly couple in his office making wills for the first time. On reflection, he tells us, he wished he hadn't said to them: "Which one of you wants to go first?"

WE ONCE heard a Glasgow chap declare: "Aye it was rough where I was brought up. If you bought a telly you put the cardboard box in yer neighbour's bin so that it was his hoose they robbed."

NOT EVERYONE has a kind word about traffic wardens. Reader Jim Fitzpatrick tells us the gag: "As the coffin was being lowered into the ground at a traffic warden's funeral, a voice from inside could be heard shouting, 'I'm not dead! Let me out!' But the minister replied, 'Sorry pal, I've already started the paperwork.'"

THE 999 emergency call system – the first of its kind in the world – celebrated its 75th anniversary. But as a reader tells us: "I phoned them up to wish them happy birthday, but they were very grumpy about it."

READERS frequently tell us conversations overheard on buses, and Sheriff J.P. Murphy remembers in the fifties on a Glasgow bus a woman declaring: "See ma man? See's maw? See chips? Cannae staun' them."

Ever since he has told young lawyers to think of that when framing written pleadings – all the facts are there and not a word wasted.

FORMER GLASGOW police officer turned novelist Karen Campbell was speaking at Wigtown Book Festival, discussing crime scenes and bodies with TV forensic anthropologist Professor Sue

Black. It reminds Karen: "We got a call to attend a report of a noisy party in Townhead. When we got there it turned out the party was a three-day wake, which had spread out into the street.

"Unfortunately the mourners were having such a good time they'd got the body out of the coffin and were dancing with it. Happy days."

WE HEAR that Glasgow cops had an unusual late-night case when a couple reported they had found a guide dog without its owner.

Arriving at the scene in the city centre, the officers did not have to look very far for a lead. The only other person in the street was a blind man, six feet away, shouting for his best friend.

RETIRED police officer Alan Barlow in Paisley recalls: "I had to interview civilians for jobs with the police, and they were asked: 'Have you ever been in trouble with the police?' Most answered no, but one guy said yes. He explained that he had had a slight disagreement with an official at the Broo.

"We were surprised that this would involve the police and after thinking it over he said, 'Maybe it was the knife.' Needless to say he didn't get the job but I checked him for outstanding warrants before he left."

A READER in the douce Renfrewshire enclave of Kilmacolm tells us the village's gentility was stirred by the arrival of three police cars and the police helicopter overheard. Someone, it seems, had reported a strange man in nearby woods with a gun in his mouth.

The panic was over when they discovered it was in fact a local piper practising his chanter in said woods.

RETIRED police officer Gerry MacKenzie recalls: "I'm reminded of the troops' toilet in Garscadden Police Office in the early 1970s. Our redoubtable cleaner had placed directly above the toilet seat a notice which said, 'I aim to please. You aim too, please. Betty.'"

MUCH COMMENT in the tabloids about the Metropolitan Police lending an old police horse to former *Sun* editor Rebekah Brooks.

As reader Bruce Skivington explains: "When they lent her a horse because she wanted to go hacking, I don't think they realised it was their phones she meant."

OUR TALES of justice in the more minor courts of Scotland remind Bill Lucas: "A tinker who made regular appearances at the Burgh Police Court in Stornoway was fined £3 by John (the Barber) Macleod, one of the police judges. Afterwards the clerk remonstrated that the same tinker had been fined £3 for a breach at the last sitting, and that this time it should at least have been a fiver.

"But John told him, 'You see every time he gets fined he comes down to the shop to sub the money from me and I knew I had only £3 in the till.'"

OUR COURT tales remind retired *Herald* journalist Ian Sharp of the procurator fiscal telling the sheriff that when cautioned and charged the accused replied: "Get me Beltrami," a reference to the famous criminal lawyer Joe Beltrami.

Says Ian: "The sheriff leaned from the bench and asked: 'Was that an admission of guilt, Mr Fiscal?'"

A MILNGAVIE reader on the bus into Glasgow realised that some folk live in a different world from him when he heard a young chap tell his pal on the bus: "Ma phone was dead for two days as I'd lost the charger."

"Everyone thought I was in the jail."

JOHN BANNERMAN was standing in the queue in a Kilwinning bakery when a traffic warden came in and took two cartons of milk from the chill cabinet.

"Have they run out of blood?" a chap in the queue asked.

EVEN WHEN confronted by the law, Glaswegians feel the need to make a joke. Former detective Gerard Gallacher tells in his autobiography *Gangsters, Killers and Me* of accompanying Belgian detectives to Balornock to confront a thief accused of robbing stores in their country. A Belgian officer asked the accused in his quaint English: "Are you a member of a club of international cash register thieves?"

The Balornock chap merely replied: "No, I am no longer a member of that particular club. I let my membership lapse as the renewal fees were far too high."

ON ST ANDREW'S Day, many Burns clubs hold dinners almost as a warm-up to the January occasion. Matt Vallance in Ayrshire recalls the late Kilmarnock Sheriff R.N. Levitt speaking at a local St Andrew's dinner. He stated that when he first arrived in Kilmarnock the trades people all lived above their premises.

"Today," he continued, "they all live in Troon – above their income."

A CANADIAN delegate to the Robert Burns World Federation annual conference in Peebles was discussing connections with

Scotland, and said a police officer from Aberdeen was once interviewed for a similar post in Calgary.

When a member of the interview panel asked: "How would you disperse an unruly crowd?" the Scottish constable replied: "Well back home in Aberdeen, an officer would remove his hat, motion to take a collection, and say they were collecting for the station Christmas party."

OUR STORY about the Aberdonian applying to become a police officer in Canada reminds an Ayrshire reader of when he worked in the mines which were facing closure, so he called in at his local police station where he told the desk sergeant he had "half a mind to become a police officer."

The sergeant replied: "Aye son, that's about all you will need to join the force."

READER John Bannerman was at Greenock bus station when he watched a ned pull up his trouser legs, exposing a pair of ladies kneelength leather boots, still sporting price-tags. The shifty chap then pulled them off and put on a pair of scuffed trainers he had in a plastic bag.

In certain parts of the country, muses John, you would assume the chap was a cross-dresser. Sadly in Greenock he was more likely to be a shoplifter.

AFTER A READER suggested on the Letters Pages that Scottish courts should sit in the evening, Sheriff J.P. Murphy, tells us: "Of course this has been tried. A pilot scheme in Dumbarton some years ago was not a success.

"The public did not turn up. Among the explanations for non-appearance were, 'I would have missed Coronation Street', and 'I was afraid I'd get mugged at the bus stop.'"

RETIRED Glasgow police officer Harry Morris, in the latest instalment of his Harry the Polis series of books about the force, tells of the ned from Govanhill who called Gorbals police office and said: "I just saw a poor old woman fall over on the ice today, right outside the chippie.

"At least I think she was poor. She only had £1.20 in her purse."

RETIRED Glasgow Sheriff J. Irvine Smith has often featured in the Diary, so we are pleased to discover in his autobiography, *Law, Life and Laughter*, that he did indeed once tell a felon, when finding him guilty, that he was a "fecund liar".

The good sheriff had misgivings that the chap did not understand him, but his solicitor reassured Irvine afterwards that while his client did not know the word 'fecund' he knew one which sounded remarkably similar, and had told his solicitor that it was the first time in his criminal career that he had heard the bench using language which he could really understand.

INCIDENTALLY, Sheriff Smith also recalls that a chap he found guilty had to return later for sentencing, but the case was taken by Sheriff Laura Smith, who had just been appointed to the Glasgow bench. The aggrieved accused, after receiving a tough sentence, told the officer taking him to the cells: "It was supposed to be Irvine Smith who was to come in the day, but he couldnae come, so he sent his wife!"

OUR COURT tales from the autobiography of Glasgow Sheriff Irvine Smith remind a lawyer of another sheriff who was asked by a nervous jury member if he could be excused duty as his wife "was about to conceive."

The sheriff was momentarily taken aback until he replied: "I believe you mean 'deliver'. But either way, you should be there."

FORMER Met detective Jock Murray, originally from Lewis, tells in his just-published autobiography, *The Whaler of Scotland Yard*, that more than 50 years ago he had sat a medical carried out by a wizened Harris doctor, Iain MacIntosh, in order to serve on whaling ships. When a fellow whaler, says Jock, went to Old Mac for advice on dealing with a cold, he was told by the doc: "Buy a bottle of rum, two oranges, and a glass.

"Place an orange on both the bottom bedposts. Keep sipping the rum until you see three oranges, and then you should be cured."

A LONDON correspondent phones to tell us: "There was some confusion in Tottenham on Saturday night about the clocks going back.

"Some folk were asking if the flat screen TVs had to be returned as well."

DO WE believe the chap in the Glasgow pub who said he got pulled over by traffic cops who told him it was stupid of him to drive so fast when it was teeming down. He claims he replied: "Who's stupid? I'm dry in my car. You're the one standing in the rain."

11
When The Stars Come Out

CLYDEBANK comedian Kevin Bridges became one of the fastest-selling stars at Glasgow's SECC when tickets for three shows sold out in two hours

We liked young Kevin's reaction when the BBC announced he would be starring in his own TV series. Said Kevin: "It'll be great to see something on national TV made from Scotland that doesn't have an appeal for witnesses before the closing credits."

AT THE EDINBURGH Fringe, Juliette Burton, from the comedy show *Rom Com Con*, says she enjoys handing out leaflets for her shows. However she recalls from last year: "Taking a tea-break in a cafe I noticed at the next table an elegantly dressed man. Around his neck he wore a large lanyard that read clearly in bold letters, 'Don't flyer me. I'm not here for the Fringe.'"

TALKING of the Fringe, even Edinburgh can seem a scary place if you are not from Scotland. Suky Goodfellow, who appeared in Back to School at the Pleasance, got lost in the Meadows in the dark on her last trip to Edinburgh.

She was finally redirected in the rain by a dog walker to where she could catch a bus to Leith, and then got lost in Leith. She got further directions in Leith by a local with more scars than teeth. Suky reassured herself by thinking: "He was perfectly pleasant, so I assume he got that cut across his nose rescuing a puppy from drowning and had donated his teeth to a charity auction for a children's hospice."

MICHAEL REDMOND, whose show *Mannequins, Fishmongers, Guacamole and Me* was at the Gilded Balloon, was filming in a Glasgow west end restaurant with a female mannequin for part of his act about sharing a flat with said model.

Says Michael: "I was acutely aware of the inquisitive stares of the other customers, and I overheard an elderly woman say to her friend, 'She looks a bit young for him.'

"Her friend looked embarrassed and said, 'She's just a mannequin. I think it's a bit of a joke', to which the elderly woman replied, 'Yes, but even still.'"

WE MENTIONED the National Library of Scotland marking its exhibition, Scotland at the Cinema, by asking for famous film quotations as if they had been delivered in Scotland.

Readers put forward:

"The names Bond, Flute Bond." (Alan Graham, Cumbernauld).

"Ah wanted to be a conductor." (Carl Williamson, Largs).

"Ye hud me at howzit gaun." (Morag Keith).

"I see drunk people!" (Keith McClory, Houston.)

"Haw, Sam, gauny gie's thon wan the burd likes?" (Ian Duff, Inverness.)

"You cannae handle Big Ruth!" (Anne Gilbride).

"A boatle o' Irn Bru. No' shaken or stirred mind, or it'll gush oot the tap." (Craig Robertson)

"It's a hunner an' six mile tae Glesca. We've got half a pack o fags. It's dark, and fit are these funny dark glasses for?" (David Grimmer).

"You've goat to ask yersel 'Do you drink Buckie?' Well do you, ya wee ned?" (Anne Gilbride).

"I love the smell of scones in the Morningside." (Fraser MacDonald).

"The first rule o' square go club, is ye haud yer wheesht aboot square go club." (Euan Smith).

"Maybes aye, maybes naw, that is the question." (Andy Ewan).

THE BIG HIT at the Glasgow Imax cinema is the Batman film, *The Dark Knight Rises*, whose opening scenes were filmed in Scotland. In the queue to go in, one fan told his pal: "They even filmed some scenes in Glasgow."

"So who's the baddy this time? The Yoker?" he replied.

FORMER COLLEAGUE Jimmy Watson recalls harmonica virtuoso Larry Adler telling of the time he lived in Paris where he saw a John

Wayne western in which the great man swaggered into a saloon and snarled at the barkeep: "Gimme a shot of redeye."

Beneath in French was written: "Une petite Dubonnet, s'il vous plait."

AT A MAIN STREET Blues gig at Edinburgh's Jazz Bar, the band announced that their CD was available to buy on the way out. According to John Robertson, the singer went on: "We won't skin you – it's only a fiver, the price of a couple of beers!"

"No' in here," came the instant reply, and loud enough for the bar staff to hear.

COMEDIAN Jeff Leach, at the Gilded Balloon with his Fringe show, Boyfriend Experience, told the audience about feeling heartened by his arrival into Edinburgh. "As the train pulled into Waverley Station I saw solar panels and I thought, that's Scottish optimism."

SCOTS crime author Ian Rankin, looking back on 25 years of his famous detective, Rebus, at the Edinburgh Book Festival, recalled his favourite pun, included in one book when Rebus was driving home to Fife, and remembering the days when smoke used to billow from the chimney tops.

The line? "It silenced him, the silence of the lums."

COMEDY rapper Abandoman asked audience members during his Fringe show, *Party in the Key of C Major*, to shout out a rule they disliked at work. While one chap objected to not being allowed to print in colour, and another felt irked by not being able to use the photocopier at lunchtime, one woman put up her hand and said the rule she disliked most was not being allowed to leave work early.

"What do you do?" asked the comedian. "I work for myself," came the reply.

OUR STORY about the collection of journalism by Arnold Kemp, *Confusion to Our Enemies*, being published, reminds a reader of Arnold telling him the story of when he worked with the extremely erudite drama critic Charles Graves, who was sent out to review a Cliff Richard concert in Edinburgh.

Arnold recalled that Graves devoted most of the piece to the jugglers who were second on the bill, making many scholarly references to the history of their art.

Poor Cliff was then only mentioned in the last paragraph which was then removed in the composing room in order for the review to fit, leaving puzzled readers trying to work out why Cliff Richard did not feature in a review of his show.

FOR WOMEN not interested in the European Champions League final, there was former Socialist MSP Rosie Kane – the one who was sworn in with writing on her hand – doing a charity performance at the Tron Theatre. We liked her description of her

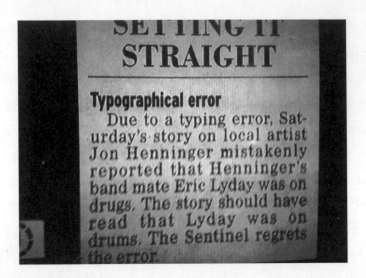

SETTING IT STRAIGHT

Typographical error
Due to a typing error, Saturday's story on local artist Jon Henninger mistakenly reported that Henninger's band mate Eric Lyday was on drugs. The story should have read that Lyday was on drums. The Sentinel regrets the error.

Glasgow roots: "We were a large family . . . like the Osmonds, but with fillings."

COMEDIAN Ben Verth, appearing at the Beehive Inn in Edinburgh's Grassmarket during the Fringe, lives in Edinburgh, so already the locals were giving him comic potential for his show.

Only the other day he was in a cheesemongers in Stockbridge when a posh elderly lady expressed dissatisfaction with the way the young assistant was cutting her cheese, and came out with the memorable line: "Look, are you new? Because I've never seen anyone so cavalier with cheddar."

WE CANNOT pass the retirement of legendary Lanarkshire singing duo The Alexander Brothers without repeating the oft-told yarn of the kilted brothers entering Canada on one of their many singing tours and being asked at passport control whereabouts in Scotland they were from.

"Cam'nethan," said Jack, only to be interrupted by Tom, who said: "Ach, Jack, he'll no' know where Cambusnethan is," and turning to the officer, announced: "Wishae."

DAMSEL SOPHIE, who brought her one-woman comedy cabaret Hot to the Edinburgh Fringe after a sold-out run at the Adelaide Fringe, tells us that Edinburgh audiences can be a bit restrained in their praise.

After one Edinburgh show an audience member said to her: "Thanks for that. My friend really enjoyed it."

A CHARITY night was held at the Citizens Theatre to mark TV and panto star Johnny Beattie's 60 years in showbiz, with appearances from Alan Cumming, Una McLean and the Alexander Brothers. We well remember sage advice Johnny gave us years ago.

"Ages and wages," said Johnny, "theatre folk never discuss either of them."

ACTOR and comedian Des McLean has lost ten pounds in order to appear as maverick politician Tommy Sheridan in Ian Pattison's black comedy I, Tommy at Glasgow's King's Theatre. To achieve that, the once chubby-cheeked impersonator hired a personal trainer who dragged him through the pain barrier exercising every day.

"There were times," says Des, "when I wished it was Alex Salmond

I was playing instead, as I would then have an excuse to go on the kebabs all week to get the right look."

AWARD-WINNING comedian Christian Schulte-Loh, performing his solo show *Stop Laughing, I Am German!* at Blackfriars during the Glasgow Comedy Festival tells us about a friend who did a gig in Leith as part of the Free Fringe during the Edinburgh Festival. Says Christian: "All forty audience members were laughing, applauding, enjoying the show, but when he looked in the donation bucket afterwards there was only £1.45.

"He was so disappointed, but when he told a Scottish comedian about it our Scottish friend says: '£1.45? In Leith? They loved you!'"

READER John Dyer declares: "Radio Clyde is running a competition to win either a £100 shopping voucher or two tickets to see an Elvis tribute act. I don't know whether to press 1 for the money or 2 for the show."

OUR MENTION of a Radio Clyde contest reminds David Macleod: "Do you remember in the days when you had to send your answers in by post, and Radio Clyde asked which pop superstar had the real name Marie McDonald McLaughlin Lawrie? The answer had to be sent to 'Radio Clyde, Lulu Competition, P.O Box ...'"

GLASGOW'S Citizens Theatre appealed for unwanted pianos for their production of King Lear. Composer Paddy Cunneen created new instruments with their inner workings.

Our contact in the performing arts tells us that the audience at one piano recital he attended was appalled when a mobile phone rang. However without missing a note the soloist merely called out: "If that's my agent, tell him I'm working."

IN GLASGOW for the comedy festival, satirist Rory Bremner was in George Square where he was quite taken with the latest temporary tourist attraction. "Get that new ferris wheel!" he exclaimed. "You're like Vienna with Greggs."

WELSH comedian Bennett Arron, appearing at Brel in the west end in the Glasgow Comedy Festival, discovered there was a party of six teachers from Holland in the audience, and he asked them if they had paid for their tickets individually. There was some feverish discussion among the teachers before one of them triumphantly announced: "Ah, you want to know if we went Dutch!"

NOT EVERYONE who is involved in the Edinburgh Festival just goes for the artistic pursuits. A reader points us to an internet discussion about waking up with a hangover: "Was working at the Edinburgh Festival fitting up the Pleasance courtyard. After a night out in Whistlebinkies, woke up dressed as a pirate. Hook, hat, beard, sword, eye patch, the whole lot. Still don't know how or why this happened. Still called Pirate Andy."

ONE POPULAR artist who no longer wakes up with a hangover is Billy Connolly. We like his explanation on the website of the Glasgow Art Club on Bath Street, currently on a membership drive, where Billy states: "The Glasgow Art Club sold me an inordinate amount of alcohol and then the b******* banned me for unruly behaviour, but being renowned for my kindness and compassion I forgave them and since my reinstatement I have spent many happy hours in their salubrious surroundings dunking digestive biscuits in my camomile."

Changed days from singing about Irn-Bru to cure a hangover.

THE Diary story of the comedian chatting with the Dutch audience members at the Glasgow Comedy Festival reminds John Park in Motherwell: "Last year at the festival we were in a bar when a mediocre comedian started asking the audience what they did for a living. One bloke in the front row replied, 'I'm a stand-up comic. What do you do?'"

OUR MENTION of Clydebank comedian Kevin Bridges' new series on BBC leads to a reader showing us a web page where the merits of Kevin were being discussed. Someone from Glasgow added the surreal comment: "I missed my Christmas dinner because of Kevin Bridges. I was in O'Donnell's on Christmas Eve and he asked me to watch his pint so he could go for a smoke. Three days I waited and he never came back. It was flat by the time I drank it."

NEWS STORIES of comedian Billy Connolly walking off stage at concerts in England, unhappy with hecklers, remind John Park in Motherwell of seeing Connolly in Glasgow. Says John: "A bloke in the audience started heckling him. Billy looked over at him and said, 'I don't like getting interrupted at work. How would you like it if I came into your workplace and told you how to sweep up?'"

OUR MENTION of Billy Connolly dealing with hecklers reminds Richard Fowler in Kilwinning: "My late friend, Phil Todd, was proposing the Immortal Memory at a Burns Supper in Kilmarnock when a member of the audience who had over-imbibed began heckling. Phil ignored him for some time but eventually looked directly at the heckler and said, 'God surely wasted a good backside there when he put teeth in it!'"Phil was never heckled again – that night or thereafter."

DEALING with hecklers continued. Jimmy frae Paisley tells us: "The late folk singer and raconteur Danny Kyle once admonished a heckler by suggesting he should 'Sit against the wa' – that's plastered tae.'"

HECKLES continued. We mentioned the late acerbic folk singer Danny Kyle and his dealings with hecklers. Jack Wright in Glasgow recalls Danny once telling a chap who shouted out: "The last time I saw a mooth like that, there was a hook in it."

OUR TALE of the late folk singer and raconteur Danny Kyle putting down a heckler prompts Brendan Ferguson in Ayr to recall another example of Kyle's mastery of the craft.

Says Brendan: "I once heard him deal with a heckler during a gig at the University of Glasgow with the classic put down: 'Yer like a lighthouse in the desert – brilliant but useless.'"

HECKLING continued. A reader tells us about an English comedian at a gig in Glasgow who was being interrupted by an incoherent drunk. "This is what happens," the comedian told him, "when cousins marry."

FOLK SINGER Danny Kyle continues to be fondly remembered. Says reader John Hart: "We were at a concert when Danny asked the audience to sing a very simple song with him. The words he told us were 'Soap, soap, soap, soap,' etc. After the somewhat bemused and embarrassed audience finished singing, Danny announced, 'Thank you for these few bars of soap.'"

BROADCASTER Dougie Donnelly, presenting the Law Awards of Scotland at Glasgow's Hilton Hotel, recalled that he himself achieved a law degree at Strathclyde University before working in radio. "I was telling the wife," he reminisced, "that when I was at Strathclyde studying law, never in my wildest dreams did I imagine that I would one day present the Scottish Law Awards.

"She told me that, funnily enough, I was never in her wildest dreams either."

OUR BEST wishes go to boxing promoter Alex Morrison, whose gym in the east end of Glasgow went up in flames. We remember Alex telling us that when 6ft 3in, black heavyweight champion Frank Bruno officially opened the gym, Alex and some friends took Bruno out for dinner, where a woman asked for his autograph.

She returned to her table where her pal, not a boxing fan, thought someone in her family might want his signature, and came over to the table of six average-looking Glaswegians and Bruno, loudly asking: "Which one of you is Frank Bruno?"

IT'S THE SCOTTISH Comedian of the Year final at Glasgow's Pavilion Theatre. We remember one of the finalists, Martin Bearne, once telling us: "If I had a pound for every time I went to the gym, I'd ... I'd be able to use the lockers."

NOSTALGIA alert as it is reported that the Stenhousemuir firm which makes McCowan's Highland Toffee has gone into administration, threatening the future of the iconic brand which featured in so many corner shops' penny trays.

Inevitably we are reminded of the Chic Murray line: "So there I was lying in the gutter. A man stopped and asked, 'What's the matter? Did you fall over?' So I said, 'No. I've a bar of toffee in my back pocket and I was just trying to break it."

FRANCIS ROSSI of Status Quo, on a music site which lists bands' worst gigs ever, proposed Dundee in 1969, where he recalled: "This fight broke out. I'd never seen anything like it – 1500 people, everybody punching everyone else: men punching men, men punching women, women punching men, women punching women – it was like the Wild West.

"Luckily someone told us to get our stuff and get out. We didn't argue, we just left. We came back in the morning and about 20 washerwomen were there in a line, on their knees, scrubbing the blood out of the lovely new parquet floor."

Worst gig? Folk in Dundee would describe it as a great night out.

PROFESSOR David Purdie, a guest speaker at the Trades House dinner in Glasgow, was actually on duty the night comedian Chic Murray was brought to the Western Infirmary for a check-up after he was found slumped halfway out of his car parked outside his house.

David's junior doctor, after checking him over, reported that Chic was suffering from an overdose. A surprised David asked him what Chic had overdosed on.

"Hospitality," replied the junior.

THE BIG NEWS for music fans of a certain age is that Cream bassist Jack Bruce was appearing at Celtic Connections in Glasgow. It reminds us of the story about Radio 1 DJ John Peel and his producer John Walters being slipped four little pink pills by Bruce when they told him they were going to see him play.

Walters threw them away and years later told Bruce that he and Peel were not big enthusiasts for drugs.

"Drugs?" says Bruce. "They were earplugs."

TELEVISION producer John Fisher has just written the affectionate book *Tommy Cooper's Secret Joke Files*, based on the piles of scripts and jokes that the late comedian had stored away.

We can just imagine a fez-wearing Tommy announcing between bottle-and-cup trick: "I always call a spade a spade. Until the other night when I stepped on one in the dark."

Or as he once told an audience: "I'll never forget the night I made my first appearance as a comedian – don't think I haven't tried."

AND TOMMY once had a sly dig at Scots, writes John. One of the gags John discovered was: "I saw a sign on a Scottish golf course once. It said, 'Members will please refrain from picking up lost balls until after they have stopped rolling.'"

THE EDINBURGH PLAYHOUSE asked theatre-goers to confess their sins in order to win tickets to the nun-themed musical *Sister Act*. Food, it seems, figured in many sent in.

"I was making soup for my mother," admits one, "and it boiled over. It was the last tin so I soaked it up with a dish towel and wrung it out into the bowl."

Mum will be pleased. And for those thinking of a trip to the chippy, another confesses: "Once when I worked in a chip shop, a moth flew into the frier. We immediately fished it out, but served it along with fish and chips to a horrible, obnoxious, regular customer."

KILT-WEARING celebrity chef Antonio Carluccio opened his Glasgow restaurant by telling the tale of the young Italian boy who was told by his mother that if he behaved himself for a whole month, then Baby Jesus might bring him a bike at Christmas – the Italians prefer the Baby Jesus to Santa.

"However," said Antonio, "the boy could not imagine staying good for a month, so he took a statue of the Madonna from the house, put it in a drawer, and wrote a letter, 'Dear Baby Jesus, if you want to see your mother again, send me a bike.'"

POOR Scottish Television – always slated for spending little on making Scottish programmes. Kevin Bridges, compering the Scottish Bafta awards on Sunday, pointed over to the STV table and declared: "Look at that. They've all been to Slaters for new suits, and have booked a table at the Baftas. That's next year's programme budget blown."

FORMER *Taggart* and now *River City* actor Colin McCreadie, speaking at Oran Mor's annual whisky awards in Glasgow, admitted he must have been stopped a thousand times by fans repeating the spoof *Taggart* line: "There's been a murder!"

However he was once on the train to Edinburgh when a local man, keen to show he had recognised the actor, said rather smugly: "There's been a killing!" The chap then added: "You must hear that all the time," to which Colin truthfully answered: "No, can't say I do."

RATHER than getting excited about the Jubilee, Glasgow's Stand Comedy Club put on the show *Dishonourable Subjects* which took a more irreverent look at the monarchy. As Glasgow stand-up John Scott put it: "America's Head of State was raised by a mother on food stamps. Ours was raised by a mother on postage stamps."

EBULLIENT Real Radio broadcaster Cat Harvey, presenting Glasgow's Ben Nevis bar with the Dog-friendly Bar of the Year prize at The Dram licensed trade awards, emphasised it was for the canine variety.

She was being ludicrously self-deprecating when she joked: "I wouldn't have got into many Glasgow nightclubs over the years unless they had been dog-friendly."

12
The Real University Challenge

A STUDENT returned from his university for the summer tells us how caring the uni authorities were in trying to help students cope with the stresses and strains of university life. A large whiteboard was put up at the entrance on which was written: "Tell us what class you are struggling with and why?"

Below it someone had written: "The bourgeoisie, because they control the means of production."

A GLASGOW reader tells us the student working in the office for the summer told him: "My dad lectured me at the weekend and said that if you really wanted something in life you had to work for it.

"He then turned on the telly to check his lottery numbers."

"I TOOK on a student for the summer," said a shopkeeper in a Glasgow pub the other day. "I found him sneaking up and down the aisles dressed in camouflage gear.

"So I had to say to him, 'You've never stocked shelves before have you?'"

PETER McMAHON in Kirkintilloch is reminded by our tales of tenants of the postie delivering a letter to a west end student flat. "Having climbed to the tenement's top floor in search of the name on the envelope, he was confronted by the final door bearing a sheet of paper with a long list of names on it which had been scored out and added to over time as the transient student occupants had come and gone.

"Not finding the name he was searching for, and reluctant to try elsewhere, he merely took the pencil which was hanging on a string, added the name from the envelope, and popped said envelope through the letterbox," says Peter.

MARK JOHNSTON recalls a class at Glasgow Uni when the biology lecturer handed out plastic beakers containing acid in which to preserve samples, and told the students not to open them.

Says Mark: "My friend opened his and promptly spilled the contents in his lap. In a panic, he shouted out what had happened and the lecturer told him to get down to the front immediately. As he leapt over seats the lecturer filled a jug with water, and when my friend reached the front the lecturer threw the contents of the jug in the direction of his crotch.

"Then, turning slowly to the rest of us, he said in a bored voice, 'The acid is actually harmless, but that's what happens to people who don't listen to me.'"

TALKING of students, a West End reader swears he heard one on Byres Road tell his pal: "My wi-fi suddenly stopped working, and it took me a while to realise that my neighbours had not paid their bill.

"Some folk are really irresponsible."

AN ENGLISH gap year student tells us she was travelling on the Trans-Mongolian train from Russia into China when an official came on board who shouted in Russian, before adding in English: "Papers!" She says an unmistakable Scottish voice could be heard in the next compartment shouting back: "Scissors! I win."

IN THE NEWS were the two drunken students from Wales visiting Australia who woke up with a stolen penguin in their hotel room. We may not have picked up a penguin, but most of us have tales to tell of unusual souvenirs after a drunken night out.

We read of one former student who confessed: "In my first year I collected bollards, flashing yellow roadworks lights, etc. Sometimes there was even a 'Road Closed' sign or two. It got to the point that I could hardly move around my room so I hatched a cunning plan and later that very night I closed off an entire road with the signs and the flashing lights.

"The road stayed closed for four whole days, with annoyed-looking drivers having to reverse out into main-road traffic. Only on the fifth day did the council come and unblock it."

A GIFFNOCK reader tells us he looked at the row of DVDs in his son's bedroom and pondered: "Teenage boys – well prepared to fend off a zombie attack, but not ready for tomorrow's maths exam."

A BEARSDEN teenager was telling his pals of the magical powers of his parents after they left him home alone at the weekend. An hour after they had driven off his mother texted him: "Turn that down!"

BURMESE opposition leader Aung San Suu Kyi, after two decades of house arrest, was in Oxford to receive an honorary degree from the university. A Scot down in Oxford tells us a member of the audience murmured that she looked nervous.

"Not surprising – she doesn't get out much," replied the chap next to him.

IT'S THE FINAL of University Challenge. Or as we recall a student in Byres Road once announcing: "University Challenge – getting out of bed in the morning."

MISHEARD continued. Margaret Phin tells us: "Having been asked by a neighbour what he was going to study at university, our younger son mumbled, 'Probably graphic design.' In reply she shrieked: Pornographic design! I didn't know you could do that at uni!"

THE CONTENTS of the fridge can be one of the battlegrounds when students share a flat. We hear of one Glasgow student who, keen to preserve the cake she had put in the communal fridge, wrote on a card propped up on it: "Don't eat me."

When she returned to the fridge the following day, half the cake was gone, and written on the card was: "I don't take orders from a cake."

A RETROSPECTIVE of the work of artist Liz Knox at Maclaurin Galleries in Ayr includes a collage of mementoes from her student days at Edinburgh College of Art in the late 1960s. There is a worrying telegram from her mother which simply states: "Please phone. Very worried. Mother."

Liz has added the explanatory note: "This is what happens when you don't phone home for a whole term."

A LECTURER tells us he was at a planning meeting on future exams where a fellow member of staff produced a new set of guidance notes for students explaining what would constitute plagiarism. When she was asked if they took long to draw up, she explained: "No, I just copied them from another college's website."

TEENAGERS attempting entry to licensed premises have to show identification to prove their age, and some wily ones will use the ID of older friends or siblings. To catch them out stewards will sometimes ask them details from the driving licence or passport such as date of birth, address, or even postcode.

One tipsy teenager proffered his driving licence at a Glasgow club on Saturday and challenged the steward: "Go on, ask me anything you like."

"What's the capital of Burkina Faso?" the large gentleman impassively inquired.

A GROUP of Newton Mearns matrons was discussing the youth of today, and how grandchildren were tardy in thanking them for presents.

However one of them proudly declared: "I sent my grandson a cheque for his birthday and he came round the very next day to thank me."

As her friends looked on approvingly, she added: "Mind you, I had forgotten to sign it."

A GRADUATE of St Andrews University, now returned to Glasgow, tells us that he heard a local in St Andrews say to a posh student from England: "Haud yer wheesht!" The poor girl looked dumbfounded until she sought clarification by replying: "Audrey and yeast?"

OUR EXAMPLE of cerebral graffiti in a university loo reminds Lyn Bulloch in Rothesay who once spotted in a London art gallery toilet the artfully arch: "Dada wouldn't buy me a Bauhaus."

WE HEAR about the two chaps trying to gain entrance to a students-only club night in Glasgow when the steward asked: "Have you got anything to prove you're students?"

"Acne and Pot Noodles," one of them answered.

"In ye come boys," replied the amused steward.

WE ASKED for your student tales to mark the unis going back, and Robert Gair, now in Hertfordshire, recalls Strathclyde's halls of residence on Great Western Road in the 1960s that had coin-operated meters for the heating.

Says Robert: "An enterprising student prised open the top of his meter so he could get at the coins underneath. When they were short of cash on Mondays they would simply borrow money from the meter and repay it on a Friday. Things went well for several months until the manager emptied the meters and found a ten bob note inside one of them."

13
Puzzled By A Meerkat

PROOF that the recession is sadly hitting folk in Glasgow. A reader leaving Glasgow's Central Station heard a mendicant sitting on the pavement ask a smartly-dressed chap in a suit for "any spare change."

The suit-wearer glanced at the coin-filled paper cup at the beggar's feet, and replied: "You're probably making more than me these days," and kept on walking.

JAMIE STUART in Glasgow's east end was in his local bank branch where one of the positions was closed with a sign in the glass stating: "Teller balancing."

"Is he auditioning fur the circus?" muttered the customer queuing in front of him.

OUR COLLEAGUE Robert McNeill reminiscing about cashing cheques reminds Duncan Smith in Lanarkshire of a friend going into a bank to write himself a cheque for £15. After several aborted attempts to spell fifteen when he tried fifthteen and fiveteen, he gave up – and wrote a cheque for £16 instead.

AND THAT reminds us here of the fabled Press Bar in Glasgow when the kindly mine hosts would allow impoverished journalists to cash cheques, made out to then owner Tom McEntee, which they didn't bank until pay day.

One former colleague on the *Evening Times* was called in by his bank manager who asked, after seeing the name crop up so often: "Is this Mr McEntee blackmailing you?"

MARTIN TAYLOR on Benbecula met a producer who worked with canny Yorkshire radio quiz presenter Wilfred Pickles. Says Martin: "After rehearsals the cast and crew would head off to the nearest pub. Wilfred would always buy his round with a cheque.

"When asked why, he replied that nine times out of ten the cheques were never cashed as folk wanted to keep his signature as an autograph."

OUR TALES of cashing cheques in pubs remind Hugh Campbell of when the Nigg Ferry Hotel in Easter Ross was the only bar around for the 2,000 men working at the nearby oilrig fabrication yard at its peak some 30 years ago, and was a goldmine catering to the well-paid thirsty workers.

Says Hugh: "After a few refreshments one punter informed the owner that if he won the jackpot on the Littlewood's football pools he would buy the pub. The owner cooly replied, 'Laddy, if you ever win the jackpot, just bring the cheque in and I'll cash it for you.'"

ALLAN MORRISON in King's Park tells us: "I have a pal who works in a bank and one day a fiscally challenged chap came in to draw money from his account. He had written the cheque in pencil and so my mate asked the customer to 'ink it over.'

"He came back and said, 'Yes, I really, really want the money.'"

CHEQUES continued. Ian McSwan in Bothwell recalls the pub in Airdrie that had a prominent sign stating: "We have an arrangement with the local bank. They don't serve beer, and in exchange, we don't cash cheques."

RUSSELL SMITH was in his local bank when a customer asked for travellers' cheques. Says Russell: "Unfortunately she was unable to recall which country she was going to but remembered that it began with 'ch'.

"Prompting with China, Chile, Czechoslovakia was unhelpful, until she remembered that it was Tunisia."

MARTIN SHIELDS, now in Australia, recalls working in the cashier's office of Glasgow Sheriff Court in the early 1980s. "In the mail one morning we received a cheque in payment of a fine. On the back were several quotes from the Bible and a protest of the cheque writer's innocence. The protestant fine payer was Pastor Jack Glass who had been protesting the Papal visit that year.

"The cheque was, of course, crossed," says Martin.

DAVID CAMPBELL in Helensburgh was an RAF pay clerk in the 1960s when paying wages into bank accounts instead of cash handed out at pay parades was introduced.

Recalls David: "The local bank manager was chuffed to get a rush of new customers to whom he issued cheque books, although the use of these was quite foreign to some. He rang to tell us that he had to write to one of his new customers who was overdrawn by £20. The miscreant apologised for the overdraft, and included a cheque, payable to the bank, for £20."

OUR STORY of cashing cheques in the Press Bar reminds legendary journalist Stuart 'Bullet' McCartney of photographer Alistair Starrs frequently cashing cheques there despite having an account at the Clydesdale Bank a mere 50 yards away.

Eventually the bank manger asked Alistair why he used the pub instead of the bank for his financial transactions.

"They keep better hours," replied Alistair.

A PUZZLED Dunbartonshire reader tells us that car insurance is getting a lot more complicated these days. He explained: "You used to

just choose the cheapest quote, but last night my wife asked if I would prefer to have a toy meerkat or 1,000 Nectar points."

FORMER BANKER Cameron McPhail has written a book, *The Scottish Nationality Test*, which determines in quiz form how Scottish you are. It asks which statement doesn't reflect the attitude of the average Scottish male, and lists i) To control the TV remote is to control the world, ii) Dirty dishes migrate automatically to the dishwasher, iii) Toilet rolls grow naturally on their holders, iv) An empty milk carton goes back into the fridge and not the bin.

The correct answer being (iv) "As the average Scottish male could never be associated with milk."

RAB CARSWELL in Greenock didn't realise how bad the recession was until he read the subtitles on a BBC Reporting Scotland story on a rare bird that had escaped from Edinburgh Zoo.

The subtitles stated that "keepers feared it might be attacked by creditors."

SO CAN there possibly be an upside to the rising cost of petrol? Well, Martin Morrison in Sutherland tells us: "I had to put fuel in the car this morning.

"It was cold, windy and raining.

"Fortunately, with petrol in Lochinver now £1.58 a litre, I can put £30 worth in the car in a matter of seconds and barely feel the elements at all."

"DID YOU hear Mark Zuckerberg's advice on how to become a millionaire?" asks our man in the city.

And he answers himself: "Buy a billion pounds worth of Facebook shares."

A FINAL question from Cameron McPhail's new book *The Scottish Nationality Test*: Edinburgh's Princes Street is some 2,500 yards long. If the economically-feasible distance between panhandlers is 100 yards, how many former bankers can make a living on this street? The answer is: "Given the fees at Edinburgh private schools, no more than one."

WATCHING news of sporadic panic buying in some petrol stations, a reader sends us an updated saying which sums up the public's

reaction: "You can fuel some of the people all of the time, and all of the people some of the time, but you can't fuel all of the people all of the time."

"A BEGGAR in the street asked me for the price of a meal," said the chap in the pub last night.

"So I gave him a first class stamp."

READER David Haining tells us: "A guy in the pub was describing the haggling involved in buying his new car. After persuading the salesman to include a couple of free extras, he suggested that a full tank of petrol would clinch the deal. 'I'm sorry sir, I couldn't go that far,' replied the salesman, 'But what I will do is knock £200 off the price.'"

14
Haikus

We asked readers to submit haikus about Scotland. These are our favourites.

SCOTTISH author Des Dillon has published a book of haikus – poems of 17 syllables arranged in three lines of five, seven, and five – with the title *Scunnered*.

We like the haiku entitled Scottish Village:

You'll be accepted
when they feel they know you well
enough to hate you.

Stephen Gold suggests:

Welcome to Glasgow,
Where often our haute cuisine
Isn'ae all that haute.

Kate Gordon in Brookfield, Renfrewshire, goes topical with:

Boxin' day the day,
Thank God fur some peace on earth,
Batteries a' deid.

Writes Andrew Ewan in Dunoon:

The Munro baggers
Like their grub after a climb.
Sort of peaks and troughs.

Iain Mills:

Wee Malky's iPod
Wisnae ever aff his heid
But Wee Malky wis

Paisley, town of mills.
All gone now, like all the shops.
Save the Job Centre.

15
Queen In Rumpus At Palace

THE PICTURES of flooding on the news remind Arlene Crawford of a similar scene in Paisley a few years ago when a wee wummin rescued by rubber dinghy from her flooded street by Strathclyde Fire Brigade told a news crew: "Ah went tae see a medium last week and she telt me ah wiz gonny go oan a cruise.

"Never telt me it wid be up ma ain street."

IT WAS WINDY but dry on the Ayrshire coast on Saturday and a few folk were trying a bit of kite-flying on the beaches. An auld fella went up to one young chap struggling with his kite in the gusts and asked him in a chatty way: "Out flying your kite?"

"Naw," the young chap replied. "Fishing for birds."

DAVID MACLEOD remembers a *Reporting Scotland* reporter doing a vox pop on Glasgow street names and asking one man: "Why do you think John Street is so-called?" The man gave this some thought and replied: "Ah don't think it's any caulder than anywhere else."

ON A RARE sunny day, a Glasgow chap was telling his mates in the pub that there were a couple of wasps in his house, and he took it upon himself to get out the fly spray.

"It said on the can," he told them, "not to spray near the eyes. But how can you be that accurate with a flying insect, so I just thought, to hang with that, and sprayed the whole wasp."

WE'VE NOT had many church stories recently so a minister contacts us to say he has divided his congregation into four sections – those who are new to the faith, regular members who always turn up, those who have lost their faith, and those who are always complaining.

Or as he puts it: "Finders, keepers, losers, weepers."

WE ASKED for your tales of tenants, and a landlord swears to us that a family with six children was having difficulty finding a flat to rent as the size of the tribe was putting off landlords.

Eventually the father told his wife to go sightseeing with four of the children in Glasgow's Necropolis while he continued the hunt. At the next flat he was asked how many children he had and he sighed before replying: "Six – but four are with their dear mother in the cemetery."

He got the flat.

A READER claims he was in a party of tourists being shown around a Speyside castle when the guide enthusiastically explained: "Although the main tower is over 400 years old, not a stone has been touched, nothing has been altered and nothing replaced in that time."

"Sounds like the same landlord as me," piped up a Glaswegian in the party.

AN ARTIST of the needle and ink tells us he tattooed a chap's name on his arm only for the chap to phone in an agitated state when he got home to claim that the tattooist had "pit the name oan backwards."

"Are you perhaps looking in a mirror?" the tattooist asked. After a slight pause the phone was put down with no further discussion.

DONALD STEWART, boss of commercial property company Forrest Developments, took the missus to the cinema in Stirling to see the Swedish-based crime thriller *The Girl With the Dragon Tattoo*, but at the ticket office he could not remember the film's full title, and instead asked for two tickets for "the film with the dragon in it."

The assistant behind the desk then handed over tickets to *The Iron Lady* – the biopic of Margaret Thatcher.

TATTOOS continued. Gordon Higgins on Skye tells us: "During a rare visit to my home town of Kirkcaldy my brother introduced me to one of his friends Shug who looked a bit depressed. He explained that the previous week, while holidaying in Turkey, he decided after one

too many to get a tattoo. When asked what he wanted, he answered in a broad Fife accent: 'My name: Shug' – only to wake up sober the following morning and find the word THUG tattooed on his upper arm."

A READER in Glasgow heard some young chaps in Central Station discussing the finer points of the English language. "What does a

'back-handed compliment' mean?" one of the teenagers earnestly asked his peers.

Our reader hopes he didn't take to heart his pal's reply: "It's when you tell people they've really nice knuckles."

GOOD to know that certain old Glasgow cinema habits die hard. The Grosvenor Cinema in the West End put a message on Facebook: "Could the owner of this piece of clothing found in Screen 2 last night please put their sheepish hand up?" The picture beneath shows a black bra.

A STIRLINGSHIRE reader was commiserating with a caravan park owner who was having a lousy summer, and was impressed that the owner, having explained how much business was down, then tried a gag, telling him: "We did have one chap with a huge caravan who said he couldn't find anywhere to park it.

"So I gave him a wide berth."

MOYRA GARDNER tells us that some years ago in the west end, a very distinguished chap in tweeds was carrying an imperious, leather-hooded hawk which was sitting on his gloved hand. Passers-by were struck dumb until one wee wummin asked: "Does your budgie speak?"

CAR NEWS, and John Cochrane notices: "French company Renault have discontinued their sports model the Renault Wind in the UK.

"Probably too many people passing it."

THE GIRLY novel *Fifty Shades of Grey* is the talk of the steamie because of its racy content apparently, although that's not immediately apparent from the title. Reader Debbie Rai asks: "Is that a book about the Scottish summer?" And a Glasgow girl commented: "I think it's about my boyfriend's underwear drawer."

OUR OCCASIONAL stories on National Service remind one older reader of reporting for his stint in uniform when he had to undertake a medical, and the doctor asked: "Can you read the letters on the chart?" "What letters?" replied our reader, hoping for a way out.

"Well," replied the doctor, "you've passed the hearing test."

OUR TALE of the chap trying to get out of National Service on fallacious medical grounds reminds Frank Miller: "Some of my older colleagues in Glasgow Libraries told of one of their number who tried a similar trick to avoid National Service. When asked by the doc, 'When I speak, can you hear me clearly or is it just a murmur?'

"Just a murmur" came the reply.

"'Perfect hearing then,' said the doc."

NATIONAL SERVICE continued. Entertainer Andy Cameron recollects: "My medical was an experience. I was at the far end of a line of naked Glaswegians who were stood there like a row of one-armed bandits including a rather effete inductee from Kings Park.

"As the doctor grabbed him in the penalty box and grunted 'say ninety-nine' he replied 'wan.......two...... three.'"

WE HEAR from Kilwinning in Ayrshire where a local lady has had to cancel her plans for a lavish 50th birthday party. It was pointed out to her that having it just four months after her parents' equally lavish Golden Wedding anniversary celebrations might raise an eyebrow or two amongst the more arithmetically numerate.

THE QUEEN was uppermost in the minds of many folk during the Diamond Jubilee. Reader Nigel Robson recalls: "In London, where I worked briefly in the early 1970s, a newspaper seller's placard boldly declared one afternoon, 'Queen in rumpus at Palace'.

"Only after parting with their pennies did readers discover it related to former St Mirren and Kilmarnock striker Gerry Queen getting into trouble at his then club Crystal Palace."

OUR STORY of the woman's 50th birthday being too close to her parents' golden wedding anniversay reminds retired police officer Alan Barlow of more innocent times in Greenock when he was called to the house of a young lad who had found an unexploded Second World War shell on a nearby hillside.

Says Alan: "His mother was showing signs of distress, as was I, when I joined her in the kitchen along with the bomb. She did not fear for her life or that of her son but that the local paper would get a hold of the story as 'Me and his faither is no merrit'. Bomb disposed of safely and *Greenock Telegraph* not informed. Result."

A WORKER in a Glasgow call centre tells us he was taking down the address of a customer in Kirkintilloch, and asked him to repeat the postcode as he wasn't sure if the customer has said "PQ" or "BQ".

He still wasn't entirely sure of the postcode after the customer helpfully told him: "B for Bertie, Q for Cucumber."

GLASGOW'S Red Road flats, once the tallest flats in Europe, were scheduled for demolition. Writer Alison Irvine, who based her novel *This Road is Red* on interviews about the flats by departing residents, was told by one: "Once there was a power cut. No lights and no lift. I walked up 27 storeys.

"But I was up the wrong flat. I had to walk down again and up the other one."

"I'M ATTENDING the annual sarcasm convention tomorrow," says a reader.

"I can't wait."

AS BARBECUE smoke briefly enveloped Glasgow's suburbs, a Newton Mearns reader tells us of a sticker he saw on a car in Texas. "A backyard barbecue draws two things – flies and relatives."

THE DEMOLITION of the Red Road flats in Glasgow reminds Maggie Wood in Australia: "It wasn't a bad place to live. My mum was in a wheelchair and did her windae hingin' electronically – the concierge camera in the foyer could be accessed via a channel on your telly. Weekend nights were a bit x-rated when amorous lovers didn't realise the glass-fronted foyer didn't offer the same privacy as a back close."

JOHN DUFFY tells us an Edinburgh gag: "Two auld Edinburgh worthies were passing a palmist's in Princes Street Gardens and one went in to get his palm read while his pal waited. The first chap came out happy as Larry and his mate asked, 'Good news then?' "Aye she telt me how ah wis going to die,' the first chap replied.

"'What's good aboot that?' asked his pal.

"'Ahm gonnae be run ower by a tram in Leith Walk,' he told him."

A JORDANHILL reader was watching her husband make heavy weather of erecting Ikea furniture when she found the instructions and handed them to him, suggesting it would help if he read the leaflet. Gathering his dignity, he replied: "That's their opinion. I'm equally entitled to mine."

GOOD to see Glasgow journalist, humorist and songwriter, the late Cliff Hanley, featuring in the latest edition of the Oxford Dictionary of National Biography.

We were once told that it was Cliff, a proud former pupil of Eastbank Academy, who claimed his house was broken into and the police officer laboriously took down the details of what was stolen, pausing when Cliff included "my dux medal". The officer asked with some astonishment: "What did your duck do to get that?"

OUR STORY about television remote controls reminds Jim Scott of earlier days when folk had their makeshift alternatives. "When I was at school my pal's dad had a snooker cue with another bit of wood taped to it which he used to push the buttons on his wood-grain effect Ferguson TV. He could also use it to adjust the set-top aerial, poke the dog when it started snoring in front of the fire, and skelp us if we were making too much noise."

A BIG bear of a chap was seen at Ninewells Hospital in Dundee delighted with the birth of his son the other day.

As he held the little one up he noticed that the baby had an identification bracelet firmly attached to its ankle.

"Just like daddy!" beamed the big fella as he raised his trouser leg to show off his own electronic anklet, put there by the courts to limit his time away from home.

A READER buying a sandwich heard a young chap tell his pal that his dad "races pigeons".

"What, you mean he runs after them?" asked his pal.

"You do know you're an idiot?" the first chap, not unreasonably, replied.

TALKING of running, we are sad to report how the colourful language of Scots appears to be losing ground. A Clarkston reader moving house tells us her two teenagers were helping, and the removal man asked them: "Did your mammy promise you new gutties if you helped?" The puzzled teenagers had to ask what gutties were.

Yet it was only a few years ago surely that every West of Scotland lad named Jim Hughes was nicknamed Gutties.

AN AYRSHIRE architect was telling his colleagues: "I was at the Royal Incorporation of Architects in Scotland's inaugural awards night in Glasgow this week and came away with three awards."

He added: "Didn't win any but it'll be the last year they sit me next to the table where they keep the prizes."

THE BIBLE reading in a Stirlingshire church the other week, a reader tells us, was from Numbers where the Israelites were told: "The Lord will give you meat, and you will eat it. You will not eat it for just one day, or two days, or five, 10 or 20 days, but for a whole month – until it comes out of your nostrils and you loathe it."

"Sounds like the Atkins diet," the parishioner next to our reader whispered.

WE ASKED for your library stories, and Sylvia Russell in Lanark recounts: "I returned a tattered library book, and rather embarrassed, explained that our puppy had chewed it up, and offered to pay for it. I remarked that they must hear a lot of strange excuses, and the librarian said that a woman who came in to pay for a lost book said she had used it to prop up the head of her recently departed husband for an open coffin viewing, and had forgotten to remove it before he was cremated."

LIBRARIES CONTINUED. Judith McColm in Irvine recounts: "I worked in Kilwinning Library for a long time and I remember a lady coming in many years ago with a plastic bag full of minute particles of paper which she explained had once been a book. On investigation we discovered that the title of the book had been *How to Train Your Puppy*. We guessed the puppy in question couldn't read."

HARRY SMITH tells us: "I remember in pre-decimalisation days a friend was in his local library in Lanarkshire. An old chap was returning a book which was overdue. On being told the fine was two old pence he offered a pound note. When asked, he said he'd nothing smaller, so the librarian let him off.

"On turning away from the counter he felt a sneeze coming on. As he yanked his handkerchief out of his pocket he pulled out a load of change which scattered over the library floor."

A RETIRED librarian tells us about a girl who came in and asked where the "non-pretend" books were. He pointed her towards the "non-fiction" but has always thought "non-pretend" sounded nicer.

AS WE stamp out our final library stories, reader Mary McNeill tells us: "I have a friend who visited his library around January 25. When he asked for a book on Burns he was told to go to the first aid section. And my sister-in-law worked in a library as a student. The most interesting bookmark she found was a slice of uncooked bacon."

GLASGOW'S City Halls and the Trades House are two of the finest buildings in the Merchant City, sitting only about 100 yards apart. We only mention it as staff at the City Halls tell us about a wedding reception there last month where a woman dressed to the nines was on her second glass of champagne at the reception when a guest asked if she was a friend of Robert, the groom. "I'm the groom's mother, but his name's not Robert," she replied.

When the guest insisted his name was Robert, she asked: "This is the Trades House?" A negative answer had her scurrying off to explain why she was late for her own son's wedding.

WELL DONE to the workers out in all weathers restoring the downed power lines across Scotland. One householder in Central Scotland, who had been without power, was in his local where he praised the efforts of the workers who restored his lighting and heating. "I was surprised though," he added, "that they were Poles. I couldn't understand a word they said."

However he was corrected by a neighbour further up the bar who told him: "I met them. They're actually Geordies."

JEHOVAH'S WITNESSES: Is it just us, or are there fewer of them going door-to-door these days? Reader John Bannerman was approached by two such chaps who, after chatting for 10 minutes, asked if John had ever believed in God.

"Yes," he replied. "And when was that, sir?" one asked.

"I would say about 50 minutes before take-off, and until 10 seconds after the plane has landed," replied John.

"Even they laughed," he tells us.

OUR RECENT car showroom story reminds a Bearsden reader of strolling around a showroom when he heard a little boy excitedly asking his dad if they could have a big flash sports car, and his father patiently explaining that he would have to work an awful lot of overtime to afford it, and that would mean him being away from home, mummy and the boys, a lot of the time if he did so.

"Can we get it then?" the little one asked.

THE NOTTINGHAM couple winning £45 million on the EuroMillions lottery reminds us of the gag when Scots couple Colin and Chris Weir won the biggest every Euro lottery prize.

"Did you hear a couple who live near Largs won the £161m EuroMillion draw?"

"Fairlie?"

"Of course, you can't cheat the lottery!"

A LONDON reader tells us a chap in his local boozer announced: "Did you see that Nasa has discovered a planet with two suns? The Jocks will be livid. They don't even have one."

HENLEY BUSINESS SCHOOL compiled a list of unusual customer complaints which included a customer who complained that a delivery driver, finding no-one at home, simply pushed a curtain pole through the letterbox. The homeowner returned to find their dog pinned against the opposite wall.

And a chap who bought a dishwasher returned to the store and announced it was obviously faulty, stating: "When set to wash, water sprays, but the plates don't spin."

A MIDDLE-AGED Milngavie reader tells us he is becoming a bit concerned about how thin his hair is getting on the top of his head. It wasn't helped by his teenage son nicknaming him "Baldy".

He tells us he now feels better by giving his son the nickname 'Hereditary'.

CURRENT television programmes were being discussed in a Glasgow bar the other night where one ageing regular declared: "I'm so old, I remember when X Factor was Roman sunscreen

A READER tells us a young girl in her office was enthusiastic about having a dolphin tattooed on her bottom, but seemed a bit down afterwards.

When our reader gently enquired why, the girl blurted out: "When he'd finished he asked me if I wanted anything else done, as there was plenty of room left."

A BBC SCOTLAND reporter tells us she managed to read the name of the late North Korea leader Kim Jong Il this week without mispronouncing it. So what, you might think, but she tells us of a fellow broadcaster who read the name out as Kim Jong the Second.

OUR MENTION of odd newspaper headlines reminds Norman McLean in Ayr of seeing a picture in a newspaper of the new Moderator of the General Assembly of the Church of Scotland descending the steps of the Assembly Hall while flanked by applauding ministers. The picture was captioned "New Moderator clapped out".

16
Keeping An Eye Out

"THE DOCTOR told me I need a pacemaker," the elderly chap announced to pals in the bar of his Ayrshire golf club last week.

"But it's going to be strange having a young Kenyan lad two yards in front of me all day."

OUR STORY of the chap mixing up "homeowner" and "hormonal" reminds Dr Paul Lyden in Helensburgh: "I was talking to a research student who said she was studying postmen and postwomen to determine their state of health. When I asked, 'Why select just members of the postal service?' I got a very blank look. Turned out she had said 'Postmenopausal women.'"

A READER in hospital in Glasgow noticed the chap in the next bed had a pal visiting who picked up the get well card on the table beside him, read it and asked his bed-bound chum: "Have you been causing trouble in here?" When the patient looked puzzled, the visitor added: "Because this get well soon card has been sent from the nurses."

"I'M ON these tablets," said the chap in the Glasgow pub the other night, "which lists amongst the possible side-effects that I might lose all sense of taste."

He then added: "True enough. The next day I started watching *Big Brother* on the telly."

AN EDINBURGH reader was discussing the new book on the D-Day Landings by Ben Macintyre with an older friend who told her he was part of a group of medical officers returning to Aberdeen at London's Euston Station when rows of troops for the landings came marching in. Said her friend: "One of the docs had a glass eye. He was waiting for his paramour to say her fond goodbyes. The rest of us decided to go for a drink, telling him to keep an eye on all our baggage.

"On our return, no sign of him except his glass eye on top of the Surgeon Captain's kit with ours all neat and ship-shape around it."

JOHN SWORD at Glasgow meat market remembers his father telling him about catching the No. 2 bus in Stockwell Street with a friend who had a glass eye. When the bus drew up and the conductress announced they were full, the chap took out his false eye, threw it up in the air, caught it, and announced to the conductress: "I see there's two seats up the stair."

She let them on.

KENNY HARRIS in Edinburgh recalls: "A bit of a nutter I worked with in London had a habit of taking his glass eye out and popping it into the drink of anyone who asked for him to 'keep an eye on that' when they popped to the loo or the bookies. Unfortunately, I drank Guinness, so never discovered the offending ocular stand-in until I was three quarters of the way down my pint."

WE SAY goodbye to our glass eye stories with Alan Barlow in Paisley telling us: "A pal of mine used to work with a colleague who had an ocular prosthesis, whose surname was Love. He was, of course, known as 'The one-eyed Love.'"

HOSPITALS. They can be confusing places. Reader Allison Gillespie in Glasgow was visiting her mum in hospital with her partner when the sweet old lady in the bed opposite shouted out: "You're my daughter Mary!" Allison went over to calm her down and reassure her that she was not in fact her daughter. She thought it was all going well until she returned to her partner at her mum's bed only to hear the woman shout: "Mary! That's not your husband, you slut!"

WE'VE SAID goodbye to our ocular prosthetics stories, but we squeeze in John Paterson in Balfron who tells us about an old relation in the then Rhodesia who had a large farm, and a glass eye. Whenever he had to leave the farmhands toiling away he would take out his eye, put it on a fence post, and tell them that it would keep an eye on them while he was away.

Recalls John: "One day he came back earlier than expected and saw that one of the farmhands had carefully placed his hat over the eye on the post."

A PATIENT in Leverndale Hospital in Glasgow's south side was chatting to a fellow patient in the psychiatric care unit who was sent there under the Mental Health Act. The patient explained that he had to miss a social engagement because of his hospital stay, then added: "For once I can be honest when I apologise for missing it and tell them I was 'unavoidably detained.'"

A READER in Troon was asking his teacher pal how he coped with his recently diagnosed diabetes. "I'm so careful," he replied, "I don't even risk talking to the lollipop lady outside the school."

WE MENTIONED that folk can get a bit confused when they go into hospital. A Glasgow reader tells us: "My mum is an active member of Amnesty International and participates in their letter-writing campaigns. On admission to hospital, not wanting to be idle, she wrote to several heads of state. After writing her first letter and passing it for posting, a nurse sidled in and asked mum gently if the King of Nepal was a personal friend of hers

CRAIG KENNEDY in Renfrewshire was out buying a birthday card, and recounts: "Is it perhaps a sign of the deteriorating life expectancy in the west of Scotland that on a recent search for an age 70 birthday card in SemiChem in Johnstone the range of birthday cards did not extend past 30."

A BEARSDEN reader was chatting to his neighbour who smoked at home, as did his wife.

Says our reader: "His wife came home from a visit to the doctor. 'Bad news,' she told him. 'Doctor says I've got asthma'.

"'That's terrible', the husband replied. If he wanted to show sympathy, he ruined the effect by adding, 'That means when I have a fag you'll have to go out to the garden.'"

A READER on the 66 bus heard a young chap tell his pal that his trip to the dentist the previous day has been "really painful". When his mate asked what they had done to him, he replied: "They were playing a Phil Collins CD all the time I was there."

A JUNIOR doctor tells us about a young child being brought into accident and emergency with a dog bite. When the doc asked the kid's father if his vaccinations were up to date he said he would have to ask his neighbour.

When the puzzled doc asked why he would have to check with the neighbour, the boy's dad replied: "Well it's her dog."

Evening News
BURGLAR PRAYED ON THE ELDERLY
WEDNESDAY

OUR TALES of music played at the dentist's remind Charles Provan in Larkhall: "Before treatment started the dentist noticed on my records that I was allergic to latex and ordered the nurses to change gloves. He asked me, 'Are you allergic to anything else?' To which I replied, 'Yes, country and western music'. He duly changed the CD to Frank Sinatra."

OUR DENTIST story reminds retired firefighter John Dyer in Motherwell of being called to a house fire in Greenock where they wondered if the chap in the house had put the chip pan on – the classic cause of fires amongst the more refreshed members of the public.

John's gaffer asked the rescued homeowner: "Did you have anything on?" Coughing and spluttering, the chap replied: "Aye. I think it was Duran Duran."

A READER tells us of an elderly relative who was boasting to his wife about the advantages of getting on in years when they were in the queue at DIY store B&Q by brandishing his discount card for pensioners on Wednesdays.

His wife threw him a withering glance and pitifully uttered: "It's Thursday."

OUR MENTION of retirement being a difficult adjustment reminds Calum Carmichael: "I knew one fellow, admittedly much too used to an affluent lifestyle, who, not until well into his 60s, happened to find himself in the kitchen of his home. He turned to his wife and said, 'Here, this is a really nice room. Why don't we use it more often?'"

WE ASKED for your senior moments, and we're afraid we couldn't stop Gordon Hay in Livingston from telling us: "An old dear answers the door to a couple of earnest young men who ask if she ever thinks of the hereafter. 'Oh yes, son, all the time. I go into the other room and ask myself what am I here after?'"

SENIOR MOMENTS continued. A Newton Mearns reader was following an older neighbour into their block of flats and noticed the chap had taken two bags of shopping out of the boot of his car. In order to carry them in each hand, he had his keys between his teeth. Arriving at the door of the flats, he put down the bags and began searching his pockets for his keys. Our reader opened the door and gestured to his neighbour's mouth as he continued to frantically go through his pockets.

FURTHER to readers realising they are getting old, one Bridge of Weir dad visiting his daughter ended up in a York pub when a pop music quiz started. After listening bemused, he confessed to her that modern music was so different – he didn't recognise any of the brief excerpts.

"Dad," exclaimed his nearest and dearest, "they are playing them backwards."

AH, THE BANTER at a Castlemilk exercise class the other day.

"Whit's that yer drinkin Mary?" asked one of the participants.

"It's lemonade. The cloudy stuff. It's soor."

"Oh and ah thought yir sucked-in mooth was natural tae," was the immediate riposte.

A MILNGAVIE reader liked the positive attitude of his 90-year-old mother who broke a mirror and told him: "Seven years' bad luck, which at my age can only be good news."

SENIOR MOMENTS: A Renfrewshire reader tells us he was in the supermarket where the bill came to about £50. He handed over the two £20 notes he had, and asked if he could pay the remainder by debit card. "Of course" said the cashier who rang it up and automatically asked: "Any cash back?"

As he had no cash our reader says: "Twenty pounds" and is handed one of the two notes he had just given the cashier.

"That didn't really make a lot of sense," our reader admitted to the cashier before quickly leaving.

A MEMBER of staff at the charming country house hotel, the Best Western at Strathaven, battled to keep his face straight as an elderly lady having lunch last week told her fellow diner that when she had a migraine she "took two paramedics and lay in a dark room."

SENIOR MOMENTS, and Hugh Walsh in Dalry tells us: "I bought a jumper then discovered it was a complete misfit. On taking it back I told the girl at the returns desk it was tight on the shoulders and back, although there seemed to be plenty of room at the front. She replied, 'That, sir, is because this is a lady's jumper.'"

AND BOB JARVIE was disappointed that a jumper he bought stretched after its first wash and lost its lustre, so he took it back to Marks & Spencer in Argyle Street, Glasgow. Says Bob: "I dutifully stood in the returns queue and when it came my turn explained my disappointment to the sales assistant for all to hear.

"She listened carefully and responded, 'I understand your disappointment and am sorry for you. I recommend that you take it back to BHS as it's their product.'"

17
Budgies And Highlanders

WHATEVER happened to keeping budgies? Every home seemed to have one and now you never see them. It was always humbling as a young reporter to see a story you had written at the bottom of a cage covered in bird droppings.

Reader Bob Gardner recalls the old gag: "My budgie broke his leg so I made him a little splint out of a couple of Swan Vesta matches. His little face lit up when he tried to walk.

"Unfortunately, I'd forgotten to remove the sandpaper from the bottom of his cage."

ALASDAIR MORELAND in Troon tells us of his late father Russell managing Third Lanark in the 1930s when he recruited a miner from Ayrshire Junior football for his defensive qualities who presented Russell with his caged bird which emitted a piercing shrill whistle.

Russell hit on the idea of keeping the budgie near the pitch.

When the budgie whistled, the Third Lanark players kept going, but the opposition would stop, assuming it was the ref's whistle. But the football authorities, says Alasdair, had no sense of humour and severely reprimanded his dad.

A READER buying tickets for the Royal Scottish National Orchestra's Brahms concert was struck by the thought: "Do you think dogs ever look at an orchestra conductor and think, 'Oh for goodness sake, just throw the bloody thing.'"

FOR SOME REASON we have bounded into dog stories, and Robert Calder reminds us of the classic tale: "A Scottish company I used to work with had an office in Manchester. One of my colleagues from Glasgow moved there and took his dog into work one day. Amid comments like 'She's a lovely dog' and 'She's really friendly' my colleague suggested that they could 'clap the dug.'

"At which point they gave her a round of applause."

THEN WE debated dogs' names. A reader tells us: "I called my dog Bingo, which was fine until he ran into the Mecca hall up the road, and I ran in shouting his name. What chaos that caused among a lot of unhappy women."

BRETT CLOUGH at the Cardwell Bar in Gourock recalls a barmaid who called her black lab Deefer. When a bemused Brett asked why, she replied: "D fer dog, obviously."

THE ODD THINGS you see in Glasgow. A reader was passing by a prestigious building in the city centre where he watched a woman carrying a basket with a cat in it being escorted off the premises by two security personnel. She was loudly telling them: "I did see the sign. It only said 'no dogs.'"

SOME FOLK are actually keen to get back to work at the fag-end of the holidays, bored with the bad weather and the lacklustre telly programmes. One businessman tells us: "I just watched my daft dug chase his tail for 10 minutes and I thought to myself, 'Dogs are easily entertained.' Then I realised I had just watched my dog chase its tail for 10 minutes."

"DOGS are tough," declared the chap in the pub the other night.

"When I went home last night I interrogated our dog for over an hour, but he still wouldn't tell me who's a good boy."

A READER strolling through the Botanic Gardens in Glasgow saw a chap lying on the grass with his dog beside him, despite the temperature hovering barely above freezing point.

As he idly wondered whether the chap was ill, the prostrate man's pal strolled over and asked him if he was OK.

"Aye," the chap replied. "I'm just pretending to be deid to see if Prince here would go for help."

LEADING AYRSHIRE coal merchant Andrew Gray in Kilmarnock tells us: "We receive very few customer complaints, but this one takes some beating.

"The customer phoned to thank us for the prompt delivery, but said he had paid the driver for eight bags and only received five. I said that our driver was very honest and would not short-deliver, and asked if he had checked the bunker.

"He said there was no need as his dog hated the coalman, and barked every time he went past the kitchen window. The dog had only barked five times."

BUDGIES continued. Calum Carmichael recalls: "Professor John Sawyer, at Newcastle University, told me of a student who wanted to enter the priesthood. To get a sense of the work he paid a pastoral visit to a sweet old lady who sat him in front of a roaring fire, released her pet bird from its cage, and retreated to the kitchen to make a cup of tea.

"Happening to cross his legs just as the bird flew by, the student struck it with his shoe and the bird landed in the fire and perished in a burst of flames. Horrified, the poor fellow hurriedly left without informing the woman, and gave up any idea of becoming a priest."

WE MUST put the cover over our budgie stories, but not before Jean Miller on Arran tells us: "I remember as a young girl living in the south side, we had a budgie come down the chimney. Weeks later, after asking neighbours if they knew who had lost a budgie without success, my dad spotted an ad in the *Evening Times*, that someone had lost a similar budgie in Maryhill.

"When he read this out to my mum, she said, 'Don't be so silly, it would have to have flown past George Square, and the pigeons would have got it.' So we kept the budgie and had it for 17 years."

WE ALSO discussed laid-back Highlanders, and Jim Scott tells us of holidaying in Wester Ross when he cycled to the shop to collect his *Herald*.

"Are you staying at the cottage at the end of village?" asked the newsagent. When Jim said yes the shopkeeper asked if Jim could drop off two *Records* and two *Expresses* on his way back.

"Turned out his paper boy was on holiday," says Jim.

OUR TALES of laid-back Highlanders remind Alastair Hendry in Greenock of his pal's car breaking down in the west Highlands and it being towed to a local garage for repairs. When the chap asked when it would be ready, the owner thought for some time, then told him: "Two wee whilies."

WE HEAR of a young chef at a prestigious Glasgow restaurant, recently arrived from Barra. Out he went for Christmas drinks at the weekend, hailing a taxi after reaching an advanced state of refreshment. Unfortunately unable to enunciate, and unsure where he actually stayed, he struggled to communicate where he was going. Fortunately the taxi driver recognised his Western Isles accent and duly drove him to the Park Bar, the haunt of exiled Gaels, where he paraded said chef around the bar until someone recognised him and explained where he stayed.

THEN there's this, from Martin Taylor in Benbecula: "I heard of a man from Lewis who decided to emigrate and spent a few evenings celebrating his departure before leaving on the ferry. Two days later he returned to Stornoway and never left the island again. His nickname became Gulliver."

A READER tells us he was chatting to a friend from the Isle of Lewis in Glasgow's city centre at a busy street corner when a leggy blonde pulled up beside them in a black BMW, stepped out of the car, and told them that she seemed to have lost her way.

The Lewisman, without hesitating, replied in his Hebridean lilt: "Do you mean in life in cheneral or are you chust looking for directions?"

LAID-BACK Highlanders continued. David Russel in Penicuik tells us about a garage worker in Fraserburgh who changed the clutch on a Ford Cortina, but was faced with a number of bolts left over. Says David: "I asked if that would cause problems for the driver, and the reply was, 'Na na laddie, there was ower mony tae start wi.'"

IAN CRAIG remembers sitting in a Western Isles hostelry one summer, sheltering from the midges and rain, when an English tourist came in and asked if the taxi parked outside was for hire. Says Ian: "A gentlemen sitting at the bar replied 'Aye' then proceeded to down his hauf an' a hauf before heading towards the door.

"The expression on the would-be taxi hirer's face was a picture.

However he was reassured by the barman, 'Don't worry. Harry's the best driver in toon. All the rest are on drugs.'"

The barman was of course joking as island taxi drivers are sober, drug-free upstanding citizens.

DAVE MARTIN tells us: "I remember being in the bar of a Lochgilphead hotel when I heard one local ask another if he could borrow his car as he had some items to move.

"'What's wrong with using your car?' he was asked. 'I've lost my licence so I don't want to be seen driving it,' was the reply."

OUR TOURIST stories remind Martin Morrison in Sutherland of an Italian visitor struggling to get round the names of whiskies in a local bar – Bruichladdich, Bunnahabhain and Caol Ila spring to mind.

Eventually the barman, impatient with the wait as the chap failed miserably, did his bit for Scottish hospitality by telling him: "If you can't pronounce it, you can't have it."

WE ASKED for your drinking and fishing stories, and Colin Campbell in East Kilbride says: "My daughter, while on holiday in the far north west, spotted a T shirt with the legend 'Lochinver – a little drinking village with a serious fishing problem.'"

THE STRANGE thoughts of aged aunts. A West of Scotland reader reveals: "I was back in the Gaidhealtachd for my Auntie Katie's funeral. I was following the hearse for the mile's drive to the graveyard, when from our back seat, another of the aunties broke the silence: 'Katie's never been to the new cemetery before.'"

MARTIN MORRISON in Lochinver tells us: "My local bar has a sign in the window saying 'Cyclists welcome'. Oh aye? Well, I cycled in and got told to dismount and leave my bike outside. Some welcome."

18
Wait Till I Get My Clothes On

READER Andy Wilson tells us about a chap buying a cup of coffee on the train who told the woman pouring it not to bother with a lid. She replied she had to fit a lid for safety reasons. "I've just come back from Afghanistan, I'll risk it," the chap batted back.

A RETIRED Glasgow driver tells of the female passenger at the bus stop who shouted in to him: "Can you wait driver until I get my clothes on?"

He tells us all his other passengers were straining their necks for a look at the passenger until they realised she was merely humphing two big bags from the laundrette next to the stop.

THE FOUR women who run the BBC Scotland travel reports also send the information out on Twitter. Alas we don't know which one of them wrote: "Big thanks to Mark in the Megane who rescued me when I broke down yesterday." She then added in case there was a misunderstanding: "Car NOT emotionally."

ACTRESS Prunella Scales of *Fawlty Towers* fame and actor husband Timothy West were on the Waverley paddle steamer on the Clyde the other day – they're big fans, apparently. One fellow passenger was heard telling a pal on the boat: "She's a lot smaller than she looks on the telly."

Naturally his mate couldn't help reply: "Maybe that's the small-scale version."

WE ONLY mention a lorry catching fire on the A75 near Castle Douglas because the BBC quoted the Lancashire lorry driver as saying that when he phoned his boss to say that the load of milk cartons and pressurised cream containers had caught fire, his boss replied that it was no use crying over spilt milk.

BUSES in Scotland are often packed with pensioners enjoying their free bus passes. Reader David McVey tells us he got on the Drymen to Glasgow bus the other day and the only other passengers were a jolly group of OAP Glesca walkers. Says David: "After I'd paid and taken my seat, one of them pointed to me and said, 'There's only one paying customer on the bus. Let's show our gratitude and give him a big haun!' And they all started clapping."

RODDIE McNICOL in Bearsden recalls being on a 'booze cruise' out of Greenock with medical staff from the Royal Infirmary when he ordered a round of beers, whiskies "and a G&T".

Adds Roddie: "After about 20 minutes I had to ask what the delay was, and was told that they had problems heating the water for the tea."

A READER travelling on the bus into Glasgow the other day heard a young girl tell her pal: "I don't think my driving instructor likes me."

She then explained: "When he asked me what do you do at a red light, I told him I usually checked my text messages."

AIRPORTS can be very stressful places – which probably explains why a reader about to go through security at Glasgow Airport heard a

track-suited traveller say to her companion after studying the various warning signs: "Is water counted as a liquid?"

READER David McVey heard the West of Scotland ticket examiner on his train this week complain about doing a journey to Alloa. David felt he was being a little harsh on the Clackmannanshire toon by stating: "I mean, it sounds dead exotic when ye say it – 'Alloa' – but when ye step aff the train all ye can hear is banjos playing."

It reminds us of TV journalist Alan Whicker recounting when he was made a second lieutenant in the army and his first posting was to Alloa, he thought the emphasis was on the 'O' and that he was going to somewhere exotic in the South Seas.

WE got back on to the subject of Glasgow trams, which reminded Jennifer Wilkie of the legendary newspaperman Sir John Junor telling her of the *Daily Express* photographer many years ago who paid a tram driver the princely sum of five shillings to take his photographs of a late-night fire in Clydebank back to Albion Street to catch the edition.

Says Jennifer: "The tram wound its way to Candleriggs where the driver jumped off with the photographs and told his passengers, 'Just have a singsong amongst yerselves, and I'll be back in 10 minutes.'

"They duly obeyed."

TALKING of city transport, Irish government minister Dinny McGinley, invited by Tourism Ireland to the St Patrick's Day charity ball in Glasgow, tells us that as a student he took the boat over from Ireland and secured a summer job as a clippie on Glasgow's trolley buses.

Years later Ireland's infamous Taoiseach, Charles Haughey, boasted about being the first politician to introduce free travel on buses. Dinny interrupted him and said: "I think you'll find I introduced free travel on Glasgow's trolley buses whenever I heard a Donegal accent."

AUTHOR Allan Morrison was discussing his book *Last Tram Tae Auchenshuggle* at the Aye Write! book festival in Glasgow where he explained that the city's original trams were pulled by horses. There was no timetable, he told his audience, Glaswegians instead knew that if the manure was hot then they had just missed a tram, and if the manure was cold then a tram was due.

He struggled for an answer though when an audience member asked: "How did they test the manure?"

THE WOMAN asking the bus driver to wait until she "got her clothes on" – she had bags of washing – reminds Ian Duff in Inverness of the very, very classic, ie very, very, old tale of the auld wifey whose pulley had broken, and had called in the local handyman to fix it.

You know the one. Reminds Ian: "He did a fine job, stood back to admire his work and said, 'There ye are, hen. Ye can get yer claes up noo.'

"'Och son, ah thocht ah'd maybe just gie ye a hauf boatle,' she replied."

A GIFFNOCK reader claims he was on the bus into town when a youngster kept turning round and making faces at the chap sitting behind him. Eventually the passenger got fed up and told the young scamp: "When I was your age my mother told me if I made an ugly face and the wind changed I'd be stuck with it."

"Well you can't say you weren't warned," the boy replied.

PILOTS have become a tad serious these days and refrain from too many quips. However a Bearsden reader on an internal flight in Australia tells us the pilot announced: "The weather at the destination is 24 degrees with some broken cloud."

He then added: "But we'll try to have them fixed before we arrive."

WE do like our stories from Glasgow buses, but not everyone is impressed by their fellow passengers. A reader heard a woman disembarking from a bus in town and telling her pal: "Sometimes I think that going on a bus is like taking part in a Jeremy Kyle roadshow", a reference to daytime confessional TV apparently.

MATT VALLANCE in Ayrshire tells us about the teenage couple who made jaws drop on a Stagecoach bus by getting on board with a baby and asking for "two half singles to Kilmarnock."

With the wisdom of Solomon the driver told them: "If you're coming on here with that baby and that pram – one of you has to pay full fare."

A READER heading for his train in Central Station watched as an agitated woman went up to a chap on the concourse and angrily complained that a pigeon had used her jacket as a toilet, and would the rail company pay for her dry cleaning.

The chap calmly answered that the pigeon was an interloper from Queen Street Station, but nevertheless he would shoot it for her.

What made the scenario even more amusing for our reader was the fact that the chap, although wearing a dark suit, was not a member of railway staff but was merely heading for his train as well.

A SOUTH SIDE reader catching the bus into town claims there was a young couple at the bus stop who didn't get on the bus he was boarding. The driver looked over at them and shouted: "Are you two getting on?"

"Naw we hate each other," one of them shouted back.

WE mentioned Allan Morrison's book *Last Tram Tae Auchenshuggle* which marks the 50th anniversary of the demise of the Glasgow trams.

Allan of course has fond memories of the conductresses, and the vexed question of when you were old enough to pay full fare.

Writes Allan: "A well-dressed lady and her son were seated. 'One and a half, conductress', came a commanding voice. 'Missus,' replied the conductress looking intently at them both. 'That boy o' yours is 16 if he's a day.'

"'I'll have you know I've only been married 12 years.'

"'Listen hen,' she replied. 'Ah'm only takin' ferrs – no confessions.'"

AND ENTERTAINER Andy Cameron recalls: "A group of us on a stag night were on our way to Barrowland for the jiggin'. A caur was pulling away from the stop and Dapper Dan was after it like he was out of trap five at Shawfield.

"He grabbed the pole to haul himself aboard, but unfortunately the 'pole' was a broom handle which was being held by a passenger who was waiting to alight at the next stop.

"While we were jiggin' to Billy McGregor at Barrowland, Dapper Dan was wearing out the X-ray machine at the Royal."

DAVID YULE in Bellshill reminds us of the yarn about the chap with two greyhounds near the White City dog track trying to board a car but being refused by the conductress, who stood by the rule of only one dug being allowed aboard. As the tram moved off, the dog owner in frustration shouted: "Ye ken whit ye can dae wi' yer tramcaur!" The conductress leaned out on the platform and yelled back: "Aye! An' if ye had done that wi' wan o' yer dugs, ye wid hae been oan it!"

OH, and before any more folk tell us, yes we have heard of the conductress who was asked if the caur was going to Maryhill, but she replied, no, Dalmuir.

When the passenger protested that it didn't say Dalmuir on the front, she replied: "Aye well it says Persil on the side, but that disnae mean we take in washin.'"

THE 50th anniversary of the demise of Glasgow trams reminds former Labour MP Maria Fyfe of her father James O'Neill being a tram driver for 20 years. During the war his conductress retrained as a driver. Says Maria: "During her training there was a horse and cart plodding along in front of her, so the inspector told her to 'bell' them.

"She placed her foot on the warning pedal so gently it could hardly be heard.'Do it again,' he said. She tapped the pedal a bit harder, but

still not loudly enough. 'Oh, hit the bloody thing,' the inspector said with some impatience. So she drove forward and rammed the tram into the back of the cart."

GORDON CUBIE in Bearsden says: "My late uncle used to tell of the Glasgow woman who was very apprehensive of the tram rails in the middle of the road.

"She asked a conductor if she would get an electric shock if her foot touched a rail." 'Yes,' he replied. 'But only if your other foot touches the overhead cable at the same time.'"

WE asked for your tram stories, and Norman McLean in Ayr told us: "A young gent boarded a tram shortly after it left Anniesland Cross.

'Do you realise that I had to run 100 yards to catch this tram as it left early?' he declared.

"'See the driver,' retorted the conductress. 'He gies oot the prizes.'"

AND JOAN JOHNSTON in Wishaw reminds us: "The old ones are the best – the story goes that a wee man with a physique resembling the hunchback of Notre Dame was attempting to alight from a tram. Unfortunately half of Glasgow was trying to get on.

"On spotting his predicament, the conductress called out, 'Haud on you lot, let the wee man aff – that's no a parachute he's goat up therr.'"

AND STEPHEN COYLE in Cambuslang recalls the classic: "Tram travelling past Shawfield Stadium on a Friday evening as crowds from the greyhound race meeting are exiting. Passenger says to conductress, 'Is that the dugs comin' oot?' The conductress replies, 'Naw, that's the mugs comin' oot. The dugs go hame in a van.'"

TRAM tales continued. George Leslie in Fenwick, when a student, had a holiday job on the trams and remembers the two-hour lecture on behaviour before they began which included an inspector telling them: "An' now we come tae dugs. Ye can allow wee dugs intae the body of the caur provided they can sit on the wummin's lap.

"Ordinary dugs go up the stairs, and big dugs? Well ye can tie their leads tae the front of the caur an' they can pull us up the hills."

HAVE always liked the way folk in Glasgow thank the bus driver when they get off. A Cambuslang reader tells us of travelling into Glasgow on a bus where one woman was so profuse in thanking her bus driver that he finally told her: "It's alright really. I was going this way anyway."

OUR PAISLEY meanness stories somehow remind a reader of being on a train in which the toilet had the old fashioned warning of not flushing in a station. In very neat writing someone had added below it: 'Except in Paisley'.

TRAMS, continued. Ronnie McLean recollects: "As the caur was full, the conductress told a posh gent, in no uncertain terms, that he was

not getting on. The indignant ratepayer barked: 'Young lady, I paid for that uniform you're wearing!' To which she replied: 'Well, next time get a size bigger, 'cause this wan's nippin' the e*** aff me!'"

AND FINALLY, we must not forget that it wasn't just Glasgow that had trams. Falkirk had a route for over thirty years.

Recalls a Falkirk reader: "My grandfather claimed that the Falkirk trams were the most uncomfortable in the country. He told of a local businessman getting off at Larbert station who said he was grateful that the worst part of his whole journey was over first.

"As he dragged his huge trunk off the tram he was asked where he was going and replied: 'Hong Kong.'"

19
I Miss Glasgow

STAG NIGHTS just get further and further away. A Bearsden reader on business in Vienna was in his hotel lift with a bunch of English chaps celebrating the forthcoming nuptials of one of the party when the chap getting married was dared to ask the receptionist a stupid question.

Our reader, who holds no truck with wasting receptionists' time, nevertheless thought the question was inspired.

He hung back long enough to hear the groom ask: "This is our first trip to Austria. Where do we see the kangaroos?"

A STUDENT in Ayrshire admits that his pals are not very worldly. When he got home from an Italian holiday which included a few days in Rome, he announced he had seen the Spanish Steps.

"Is that a tribute band?" his pal asked.

THE BONDAGE bestseller *Fifty Shades of Grey* was being discussed in a Glasgow pub the other night, when one chap declared: "The girlfriend said she always had a fantasy about being handcuffed."

He added: "So when she went on holiday to Turkey I hid some drugs in her case."

I. M. SCOTT in Singapore, like any decent ex pat, was looking forward to the home-made tablet his wife was bringing back from Scotland. He gave some to his uninitiated American boss who, once he had tried it, remarked it was Scotland's version of crack cocaine, as you could become totally addicted, and it makes all your teeth fall out.

A READER in Australia contacts us: "I saw a car in Sydney with a sticker on the back window saying 'I Miss Glasgow'.

"So I smashed a window, nicked his radio, and left a note stating 'Hope this helps.'"

A KILMARNOCK reader just returned from Majorca swears to us that his holiday rep told him that Irish singer Sinead O'Connor was booked into the holiday complex. When the rep's boss saw her, he turned to the rep and told him to quickly check that the poolside quiz had no 'one-hit wonders' questions that could give any offence.

AS SUMMER holidaymakers return from foreign climes, we hear their stories. A Bearsden reader who visited Los Angeles noticed a comely young woman with strikingly long legs wearing a T-shirt with LAPD on the front. Our reader was still wondering if she could possibly be a member of the local police force when she walked past and he noticed on the back of the shirt were the letters ANCE.

BEST-SELLING Scots author Laura Marney, appearing at the Aye Write! festival in Glasgow on Sunday, once appeared at the Edinburgh Castle pub in San Francisco where the manager advised: "Scaddish it up, they'll love it."

Recounts Laura: "The clientele was mostly third-generation San Franciscans who, through some tenuous lineage on their great-granny's side, identified as being Scottish.

"To test this theory, instead of saying 'out the window' I tried 'oot the windae'. This was met with a chorus of approval.

"I decided to go Full Glesca, describing a character as 'staunin' her grun', which won rapturous applause. I realised that the more Scottish I became, the less they understood, the more they enjoyed, and so I finished with 'I'll skite ma haun aff your bahookie' and the crowd went wild."

HOLIDAY stories, and a Renfrewshire reader back from Ireland tells us the train he was on broke down and failed to leave the station. What was worse, the lights in the carriage then failed. At that point over the intercom system came: "This is the driver speaking . . . or is it?"

NEWS from Canada, where ex-pat Fay Copland – her name not the part of Glasgow she left – in Ontario, tells us a fellow Scottish exile

phoned to tell the police that her son had found a bike and wanted to report it in case the owner had reported it stolen.

After telling the police constable: "Ma wee loddie funn a bike lyin' up agin a wa' an' he disnae ken wha' it belangs tae," she was told: "Listen ma'am, I'll ask the questions. You just answer 'Yes' or 'No.'"

A READER tells us he was perusing the American website *Dumbest Laws* which dredges up amusing, if forgotten, old laws. These include pickles are not to be consumed on Sundays in Trenton, New Jersey, and you can face up to 30 days in jail for selling oranges on the sidewalk in Miami.

However he questioned the veracity of the site when he then read: "It is illegal to kill an Englishman except for pleasure. (Scotland)."

That's surely not true, is it?

GOOD to hear former Secretary of State for Scotland Sir Malcolm Rifkind on Radio 4 discussing the dangers of dodgy translations when he was Foreign Secretary. We know it's an old one, but we liked him recalling the British minister speaking in Moscow at the height of the Cold War who declared in a speech: "The spirit is willing, but the flesh is weak."

He was surprised later to see the speech translated into Russian as: "We have lots of vodka, but we're rather short of meat."

ODD translations continued. Gordon Airs in Bridge of Weir recalls: "When the Chinese published *The Grapes of Wrath*, it was translated as The Angry Raisins."

THE NEWS from America is that the CIA has foiled another underwear bomb plot, this time in the Yemen. A reader at Glasgow Airport heard a fellow traveller tell his companion who was reading the story in his newspaper: "That's all we need. It will only be a matter of time before airport security start giving you wedgies when you check in."

A READER in a Glasgow office had to pass on the observation from his boss who felt he was getting the blame for everything by head office. Or as he memorably put it: "I'm no one's escaped goat!"

READER Bob Byiers reminds us of the old yarn of the British politician arriving at a foreign airport to be greeted by a large welcoming party. Says Bob: "As the leader of the delegation made a welcoming speech in faultless English, the politician realised that he did not have enough of the language of the country even to begin his reply with the equivalent of 'Ladies and Gentlemen'.

"Spotting two toilet doors with words written on them he thought he had solved his problem. He got a somewhat strange reaction and learned later he had addressed the welcoming committee as 'Toilets and Urinals.'"

WE'VE NOT mentioned American tourists for a while, so we pass on from a reader in London who heard a chap chatting up a tipsy American girl in the pub who asked where he was from. "I'm Cornish," the chap replied.

This confused the American girl, who asked: "Is that like from Cornland?"

THE SAYINGS of bosses continued. Joe McNellis in Omaha says: "I recall an old boss who, when trying to make a point, said, 'Gentlemen, do you not see the handwriting is down the hall?'"

SCOTLAND finally had one good weekend of weather. A reader swears a chap at the golf club announced he was flying off to Switzerland shortly.

"Are you going to Bern?" asked a fellow member.

"No, I don't think it will be that hot," he replied.

WE remember a report that said that one in four Brits claims to have Irish ancestry, yet nearly half were either lying or exaggerating. It only came to mind when we heard a chap go on about his Irish roots until his pal stopped him and told him: "You, Irish? You probably think County Down is a game show on Channel 4."

ALAN LANG was in New Orleans. Walking down Decatur Street, he passed a boy of about eight tap-dancing who called out: "Hey mister. Betcha a dollar Ah can tell you where you got yo' shoes."

Says Alan: "Having just arrived in town and not being aware that M&S had opened a branch in the Big Easy, I rose to the bait and took his bet. To which he replied, 'You got them on yo' feet. Welcome to N'Awlins mister!'"

With a sheepish grin I parted with my dollar bill. Still, I suppose it was more inventive than 'Huv ye goat the price o' a cup o' tea pal?'"

THE PROBLEMS with being a Scot down south. Chris Tomsett in London, who wanted his kilt dry cleaned after attending a wedding, tells us: "I wasn't sure if the local dry cleaners would know how to tackle it, so I popped round the corner and asked hopefully, 'Can you clean kilts?' "I was momentarily confused with the reply, 'Course mate – double, queen or king size?'"

IT'S FUNNY how terms that were once so common don't crop up as much. A reader on holiday with his daughter was in an old-fashioned cafe when she went to the loo. When she came back he asked her if she found it OK.

"There was a door marked WC," she told him. "I guessed it was for women and children."

VERBAL misunderstandings continued. Russell Smith was having a meal in the former Yugoslavia when he went up to the bar and said he would like to pay.

The young barmaid, who prided herself on her knowledge of English, called a waiter over who graciously led Russell to a door marked WC.

AS ithers see us . . . A Diary fan in the US sends us this gag from his local newspaper: "I was in a pub last night and I was seated near two rather large girls at the bar. Both had strange accents, so I said, 'Hello, are you two girls from Scotland?' One of them screamed, 'It's Wales, you idiot!' So I apologised and said, 'Are you two whales from Scotland?'"

THE AURORA BOREALIS have been providing some extraordinary light displays across northern Europe. But as reader Jon Jewitt tells us: "Forget the northern lights and come to Paisley. The police helicopter searchlight gives us brilliant displays night after night, even when it's cloudy."

DUMBARTON Rock is a vast volcanic plug dominating the Clyde town, so it's only natural that the nearby bowling club is named The Rock Bowling Club. John Cochrane was in the club's car park when he was approached by an American lady who asked: "What kind of rocks do they use to bowl with?"

"I BOUGHT a Greek salad," said Edinburgh Festival favourite Milton Jones.

"It was the least I could do – he didn't have any money."

DAVID SPEEDIE in New York is used to the complicated instructions issued with products bought in the USA. So he was delighted with the simple instructions when he bought a Stirling Albion top from the club's online store that arrived with the sensible care instructions on the label 'Wash When Dirty'.

AN East Kilbride reader tells us about his daughter moving to Spain, and planning to take her pet dog with her. She was reading the British Airways website about containers to transport pets in when she suddenly wailed: "It says here that the container must be large enough for the pet to stand up, turn around and lie down."

She added: "I'll never be able to teach him all that in time."

A READER in America tells us she accidentally locked herself out of her car, but was rescued by a police patrol officer who sprung the door open with a Slim Jim – a long piece of thin metal.

Impressed by his skills, she told him that they should make versions small enough to fit in your handbag.

"They do, ma'am," he replied. "We call them keys."

A GLASGOW chap was at a sales conference in Switzerland, and when he phoned home his girlfriend asked what the view from the hotel was like.

"Picturesque," he replied. "But I don't know what Esque looks like," said his confused girlfriend.

20
Festivals

AS FOLK slowly get in the Christmas spirit, a reader told by his wife that they would be going to a big family dinner on Christmas Day, and that all he had to do was buy some wine for the occasion, couldn't stop himself from asking: "What wine goes well with stories about operations and divorces?"

CHRISTMAS shopping means men venturing into shops they don't normally frequent. A reader tells us she was in one Glasgow store when a chap asked if they had any 'crotch bags'.

The assistant, trying to help the chap out, asked: "Do you not mean 'clutch bags'?" Sadly the chap didn't grab the helpline thrown at him, and instead ploughed on: "What? Is that a bag for a car?"

THE BIBLE updated. One reader suggests the gospels should now read: "And in those days Emperor Augustus decreed that all must return to the town of their birth, that they might sort out their parents' computers."

GLASGOW lawyer Austin Lafferty was donating blood when the nurse told him she had taken her nephew to see Santa in a well-known retail centre. The couple in front told the bearded chap that their son was called Shug. Santa's face lit up and he declared: "Aw brilliant. That's ma name too!" Shug minor turns to his mother and whispers: "Ah thought his name wis Santa" and with the quickness of wit for which Glasgwegian mothers are famed, she replied: "This is his brother. Santa's oan a break."

OUR LONDON correspondent hears a local announce: "In Scotland, Christmas is celebrated by overeating and the mass consumption of alcohol. And is known simply as the weekend."

HER FRIENDS looked aghast as a woman in a Glasgow coffee shop announced: "I got home to find all the windows and doors wide open. Everything was gone. What kind of sick person would do that to another human being?" She then added: "I knew I shouldn't have left the kids' advent calendars where my husband could get at them."

THE LATEST leaflet from supermarket chain Lidl, which dropped through David McGirr's letterbox in Dunblane, has the heading:

"Perfect for Mother's Day". Below it was a 99p bottle of anti-wrinkle cream.

David may not be an expert on running multi-national supermarket chains, but he's fairly confident giving that as a present isn't going to win you any favours.

TALKING of Mother's Day, mothers can, of course, be hugely defensive of their children's abilities. One mother once defined 'a show-off' to us as: "Any child who is more talented than your own."

AT a St Patrick's Day's breakfast at the Indigo Hotel, general manager Denis MacCann tells us the Irish take their food seriously. There is a fast food outlet in Dublin serving chicken, he says, which has the claim printed in the window: "If Colonel Sanders had used our recipe, he would have made general."

WITH the Easter school holidays starting, Paul Cortopassi in Bonnybridge tells us of the primary one teacher who had her class enthralled with the story of Easter and the crucifixion. Says Paul: "She came to the part where Jesus said, 'I thirst,' and she continued, 'and guess what they gave him to drink? Vinegar!'

'The b*******,' muttered the entranced five-year-old beside her who was clearly caught up with the whole drama.

"'Quite so,' declared Miss, and carried hurriedly on."

JIM HUNTER tells us about a well-refreshed reveller at a New Year's party who got so emotional after the bells that he contacted everyone in his phone's address book to wish them a happy New Year. An unimpressed fellow party-goer asked: "Was he using oot-yir-Facebook?"

BOB FORSYTH in Uplawmoor tells us of attending a Burns supper where the chairman was teetotal. Says Bob: "He was determined to do the right thing when the piper played in the haggis, and had arranged with the hotel staff to provide him with two glasses – one with the cratur and the other with cold tea. When the moment arrived he gave a glass to the piper and took one himself and duly toasted the haggis.

"The look on his face when he inadvertently quaffed the goodly measure of whisky was nothing compared to that of the piper on scoffing the cold tea."

AN EDINBURGH reader was reminiscing about the Burns Supper he attended during which a High Court judge was giving the Immortal Memory. As said speaker liked a few halfs over the evening our reader was able to go home that night and honestly tell his wife that despite his appearance, he was "as sober as a judge."

THERE'S ALWAYS one misogynist, even on Valentine's Day. Said the chap in the pub catching a pint on the way home: "The wife just called to say that three of the girls in the office have just received bouquets of flowers for Valentine's Day and that they were absolutely gorgeous.

"I told her, 'That's probably why they got the flowers then.'"

TONI MORRISON tells us: "While my colleagues were being surprised with Valentine's Day flowers and cards from secret admirers, I was surprised to receive the following text message from my local chippie, the Atlantic, 'Celebrate St Valentine's Day with us by getting a free bag of chocolates with every fish supper!'

"If it had been a pizza or sausage supper I might have taken them up on the offer."

THE PERIOD of Lent began with Ash Wednesday. One chap in Glasgow asked if he ever gave anything up for Lent, replied: "Usually my New Year's resolutions."

THE LIST of names Scottish parents gave their children last year makes Scott Macintosh in Killearn ponder: "I trust that Caledonia's parents are not Mr and Mrs MacBrayne, Isla is not the offspring of the Harris family, River's folks are not called Forth, Logan is not the son of the Berrys, Poppy is not the daughter of Mr and Mrs Day, and pity Diesel if his mum and dad are the Lawries."

IN the shopping bedlam leading up to Christmas, Steven McKenzie was in Toys R Us in Govan when he heard a mother shout at her daughter: "Ginger! Come here."

A chatty fellow shopper couldn't resist asking the woman: "Oh is that her real name?" "No," replied the shouting mum. "It's Fiona, but it's ok she likes it. I'm getting her used to it 'cos that's all she'll hear when she goes to school."

IT WILL be amateur time in the country's boozers when office staff head for a Christmas drink. A reader recalls last year when an office group came in and the boss asked a giggling girl what she wanted to drink. She couldn't think of anything so he suggested: "Gin and tonic?"

"What's in that?" she asked.

A LENZIE reader is hoping he doesn't repeat his mistake of last New Year when he couldn't get out of his driveway because a visitor to his neighbour's New Year's party had blocked him in.

When he went to the neighbour's to ask to get the car moved he was asked inside for a drink.

About ten minutes later, as he was convivially holding a drink in the host's kitchen, he suddenly blurted out: "Oh no, I've left the wife in the car."

A READER heading home to Glasgow's south side on the train at Hallowe'en heard a chap tell his pal: "The wife's going out tonight and told me to look after any kids that come to the door.

"So a night in with the lights off, watching the football on the telly, and scoffing a huge bowl of sweets by myself. Magic."

WE FEAR the stress of Christmas shopping may already have begun. A reader at the Silverburn shopping centre heard a mother snap at her complaining young daughter: "You're forgetting mummy is mummy and not daddy. Daddy is the one who cares."

A READER tells us he used the Tory Party principle for awarding guisers who came to his door on Hallowe'en. As he explained it to us: "You give all the sweets to the richest-looking kid, and trust that the sweets will trickle down to the other weans."

"A WEE LAD," says Craig Bradshaw in Saltcoats, "turns up at the doorstep on Hallowe'en and says, 'Trick or Treat? And by the way, mister, I'm diabetic, so it's cash only.'

"Can't fault the wee man for trying in these straitened times."

OH YES it's panto time soon, and staff at the Glasgow Tron Theatre are hoping there will not be a repeat of a previous panto when the traditional throwing of sweets into the audience involved the rather large Lees' macaroon bars which had been gifted by the manufacturers.

Recalls a Tron staffer: "You can imagine the embarrassment when the sweetie-bowling skills resulted in a direct hit to the eye of an elderly audience member. To make matters worse, when said audience member was then escorted from the auditorium for some first aid treatment for her already blackening eye, she was hit in the face by one of the theatre doors, resulting in another black eye.

"Not quite the shining example of great customer service that we were aiming for."

21
A Sad Farewell

SAD to hear of the death of former Glasgow Tory councillor and later MSP John Young. A true gentleman. We always liked the story John told of when he first canvassed in Gorbals in the early 1960s. He went up a tenement close, knocked on two doors without getting an answer, then knocked on the third door which was opened only enough for a man to keek out and ask gruffly what he wanted.

John handed in an election leaflet and made the short prepared speech about hoping to get the chap's vote. The man behind the door opined vociferously that Mr Young would not get far in politics canvassing cludgies.

JOHN retained his sense of humour when he was elected as the oldest Tory in the Scottish Parliament. When he was patiently waiting to speak in the parliament, the presiding officer controlling the microphones got in a bit of a fankle and announced: "I'm sorry.

I pressed the wrong button." John merely told him: "Well, I'm glad you're not president of the United States."

SAD too the death of fiery Labour politician and friend of the Diary Janey Buchan. We remember when she was standing as Labour's European candidate, and her campaign bus was slowly going down Byres Road with the chap on board bellowing through the loud-speaker: "Vote Buchan. Vote Labour."

As usual, the speakers weren't of the best quality as the bus was stopped by the police and the Labour volunteers told they had to stop swearing. The officers thought the chap had been shouting "Vote f***** Labour."

WRITER Gore Vidal, who died aged 86, was never at a loss for words. Frankie Boyle tweeted that his favourite Gore anecdote concerns an incident when Norman Mailer punched Vidal. Vidal's ice-cool response? "Words fail Norman Mailer yet again."

MATT VALLANCE tells us about the funeral of a popular chap in Ayr where his "contribution to sick animals" was praised by a friend delivering the eulogy.

The friend then added: "But he didn't know they were sick when he backed them."

VIDAL SASSOON, the late celebrity hairdresser acknowledged the style of Glasgow women by opening one of his salons in Princes Square in the city. It reminds us of when award-winning Glasgow hairdresser Rita Rusk employed Sharleen Spiteri, now singer with multimillion album selling band Texas, as a stylist, and Sharleen came to her to say that she was resigning in order to pursue a career in music.

Rita admits she dismissed such a fanciful claim and accused her of covering up the fact that she was moving to Vidal Sassoon.

THE DEATH of sculptor George Wyllie, of paper boat and straw locomotive fame, reminds architect Tom McKay of the artist's wicked sense of humour.

"George was best man at a friend's wedding, and at the reception he presented the bride and groom with a big brown paper parcel. They eagerly unwrapped it and inside was a beautifully welded chastity belt George had made with a great big padlock and only one key."

AFTER the death of veteran Irish comic Frank Carson, reader Rob Mackenzie tells us: "I was standing behind Frank in the queue at Inverness airport when he was asked, 'Where would you like to sit on board Mr Carson?' He replied: 'As close to the black box as possible.'"

OUR MENTION of Frank Carson reminds Scottish entertainer Andy Cameron of Frank's great charity work. At one such event Frank took Andy to meet his mum, Ruby, in Belfast. Says Andy: "Ruby lost an eye when she was 60 and when we entered the house she was dozing in front of the fire.

"When Frank called out, 'Ruby here's that Andy Cameron over from Glasgow to see you,' she was startled for a moment and then she came out with the classic line, 'Oh hello Andy, sorry about that – I was just having 20 winks.'"

WE BELIEVE that Frank would be chuckling in the afterlife if he knew, as reader Colin Williams in Dollar relays to us, that BBC Scotland, in the subtitles during a news bulletin, should have reported that Frank Carson's funeral took place today at a mass in Belfast in a Roman Catholic church "where he also received a Protestant blessing."

The subtitles on the screen interpreted this as Frank "also received a prostitute's blessing."

SAD to hear of the death of Jocky Wilson, the Scottish world darts champion, who was perhaps not the stereotypical athlete. Fellow darts champ Bobby George told in his autobiography of having to share a room with Jocky while playing in a tournament in Las Vegas.

Waking, Bobby realised he was out of toothpaste, and asked a sleeping and extremely hungover Jocky if he could borrow his.

Jocky stumbled out of bed and started rummaging through his suitcase, but suddenly stopped in his tracks and shouted: "Why am I sat here looking for toothpaste for you, Bob? I haven't got any f******
teeth!"

WE ALSO recall the chap at a conference in Aberdeen returning by train to Glasgow who sat down opposite Jocky and blurted out: "Are you Jocky Wilson?"

"Yes," replied Jocky, "and are you Gordon Davidson?"

"Yes!" said a delighted, but puzzled, Gordon. "But how do you know my name?"

"It's on your lapel badge," said Jocky.

THE DEATH of Bert Weedon, whose tutorial books taught millions to play guitar, reminds Ian Brock in Bearsden of bumping into Shadows guitarist Hank Marvin and his wife in Florence where Weedon came up in conversation. Recalls Ian: "Hank's wife's eyes went heavenward. I said to her: Bert did teach the world to Play the Guitar in a Day. She replied in her Aussie drawl, 'Bedly!'"

SAD to hear of the death of retired football commentator David Francey whose distinctive passionate voice was always recognisable.

The story was told that BBC Scotland in the 1970s held a David Francey soundalike competition.

David himself secretly sent in a tape – and came third. The winner simply repeated "Jimmy Johnstone" in frantic Francey-style diction for three minutes without pausing.

AND ARTHUR CLEARY tells us: "I remember listening to his commentary at Hampden when the old press box facilities were a bit

Spartan. He was ranting on in his usual style when, without breaking his stride, he continued, 'the bench I was sitting on has just collapsed and I am staring at the ceiling, but will keep you updated as much as I can.'

"He never stopped his commentary while his bench was being lifted – a true pro."

JOHN SCOTT in Port Glasgow recalls: "David Francey was once commentating from a table at the side of the pitch.

"Suddenly there was a thump, followed by silence, then after some seconds he came back with the words, 'Sorry for the break in commentary. I have just been hit in the face with the ball. I don't know who it was, but he won't be having a very good game the next time I'm commentating.'"

WE have good memories of mischievous Govan Shipbuilders' shop stewards' convener Sammy Gilmore who died, aged 72.

He once told us that when the Govan yard was being taken over by Norwegian company Kvaerner there was a mass meeting of the workforce to decide whether to oppose it.

But Sammy said he knew the workers were willing to go along with it when one of the workers arrived for the meeting with two horns stuck on his safety helmet to make him look like a Viking.

SAMMY could always tell a story against himself. He once said he was in the pub when a fellow toper came over and asked if he was the chap from the shipyards. Said Sammy: "Of course I liked being recognised. Then he told me I would have been on the telly show *Spitting Image*, only there wasn't enough Plasticine to make my bloody nose. That sorted me."

THE DIARY is truly saddened by the death of Campbell Christie, who was one of the most decent men around.

Retired trade union official Willie Gibson recalls with fondness when Campbell, with typical altruism, took a substantial pay cut to move from his senior post with a civil service union to take over as general secretary of the STUC.

Recalls Willie: "When this was reported to a group of union officials, one of them, with the hard-to-please attitude of West of Scotland trade unionists, asked: "If someone is prepared to take a reduction in wages, is that person the most suitable to be the leader of Scottish trade unions?"

22
Putting Down The Jumpers

THE SPORTS story that held everyone's attention this year was of course the fall of Rangers. Naturally Celtic fans didn't shed to many tears.

Said one: "*Sky Sports* would like to apologise to all subscribers for wrongly advertising that they could watch Rangers in 3D. They meant Rangers in D3."

"THE ELECTRONIC equipment being tried out for goal-line technology will not be used at Rangers games next season," a Celtic fan phones to tell us.

When we asked why, he replied: "Apparently it doesn't work with goalposts made from jumpers."

RANGERS latest: a reader phones to tell us that there is further bad news for the club as Ibrox Park has not met the criteria to be a third division ground.

He adds: "It has four stands, floodlights, toilets and a flat pitch."

WHEN a young lad in Glasgow was asked by a family friend what team did he support, he answered "Rangers."

"But who is your 'big team?'" the chap insisted.

IT'S BEEN tough weather for golfers. We hear of one minister playing at St Andrews with friends who was surprised when the caddy asked if he was a minister by any chance.

As he was not wearing a dog collar as part of his golfing attire, he asked how he knew.

"I've never seen that much bad golf without any swearing," the caddy replied.

SIR ALEX FERGUSON was telling the sporting press recently that he would like to bring in one or two new faces to Man U before the start of the season.

The story going around is that when Wayne Rooney heard this, he asked if he could have one of them.

THE ECONOMIST magazine has published an article detailing the shorter lifespan of folk living in Glasgow compared to other cities, and wonders about contributing factors.

We gather one reader of the esteemed magazine is not a fan of the city, as he commented on the magazine's website: "The Commonwealth Games in Glasgow will be the first major sporting event where the crowd is on more drugs than the athletes."

FORMER Scotland footballer John Robertson's autobiography *Super Tramp* has been published in paperback by Mainstream. In it, John recalls being at the Excelsior Hotel with a Scotland squad under the stern managership of the late, great Jock Stein. John had repeatedly asked the comely receptionist what time she finished her shift, and eventually she gave in and said she would be in room 402.

Writes John: "I went to the room and knocked but there was no answer. I went to my room and asked the night porter to ring 402 and to my horror he said: 'You want to speak to Mr Stein as this time of night?'"

OUR MENTION of advice from golf pros reminds entertainer Andy Cameron: "I started playing 42 years ago and went to Stephen Bree at Cathkin Braes for a series of lessons which helped me tremendously, although I doubt if they helped Stephen very much.

"I always remember his tip: 'You should think about cutting 18 inches off your clubs.'

"When I asked if this would help my swing Stephen said: 'No but it'll make it easier for you to get them into the bin.'"

WE HAVE mentioned before the cheeky owners who have tried various ruses to have their racehorses registered with the occasional rude name.

Foster Evans points us to the race card at Down Royal near Lisburn the other day where Rachel O'Neill's horse Xilobs God came in seventh at 25/1. An unusual name indeed, until you read it backwards.

THE WORLD football organisation Fifa has an article in its newsletter about funny episodes at games, and, guess what, the only one which mentions a Scotland player, involves drink. Step forward St Mirren player Stevie Thompson whom Fifa recalls: "Thompson gave into temptation during a 2009 pre-season friendly between his club Burnley and Portland Timbers in the USA. After falling over the billboards, Thompson came to rest by a stall promoting beer.

"'I landed on this person's table and I just instinctively grabbed this guy's pint and had a drink,' the player said."

Naturally he was capped by Scotland.

AS THE OPEN got under way at Lytham & St Annes, an Ayrshire reader told us that there were still a few old chauvinists around at one or two golf clubs. He was in the bar at his own course when a senior member declared: "Golf! The only occasion when a man should have an iron in his hand."

NEWS about the 11-year-old boy who flew to Rome from Manchester without a ticket or passport. Our football contact tells us: "The good news for him is that after making it into Europe without spending any money he's being offered the Motherwell manager's job."

THE COMPLEX financial problems of Scottish football linked to the demotion of Rangers were being discussed by some locals. Eventually one chap tried to explain it: "As the late great Bob Marley once sang, 'No Rangers, No Sky.'"

GOLF legend Tom Watson, now in his 60s, unveiled a plaque on the 18th fairway at Turnberry to commemorate his 1977 Open victory. We always liked Tom's comment in an interview when he explained: "As a young man I enjoyed being around older people more than younger ones. I thought they had so much more to offer. I don't hang around older people as often these days. They're getting harder to find."

ONE cynical observer of the Rangers machinations declared: "Playing Rangers Monopoly with the kids. If you go bankrupt you exchange your token for another, transfer all assets, get cash and start again."

THE SCOTTISH Junior Cup final was played in glorious sunshine at Almondvale between Shotts Bon Accord and Ayrshire favourites Auchinleck Talbot. At one point two comely blonde ladies, a bit scantily clad due to the searing temperatures, were watched by fans heading to one of the stands, and there was a discussion about which team they supported.

"They can't be from Auchinleck," opined one football seer.

"Why not," asked his mate. "No tattoos," he replied.

CUP final fever in Edinburgh, where the Luath Press has re-released the book of fans' memories entitled *We Are Hibernian* in which we learn that the Proclaimers have always kept the cup final date clear from any gigs every year just in case, despite the mocking of non Hibees.

And singer Fish – remember the Hibs top is green with white sleeves, and the Arsenal top red with white sleeves – recalls: "I also loved Arsenal, because you could buy Arsenal videos, turn the colour down, and watch Hibs play really well in Europe."

WHATEVER happened to The Diary's occasionally disparaging view of Kilwinning, a reader asks. Well, we hear the route of the Olympic torch through Ayrshire to Glasgow deliberately avoided Kilwinning.

The organisers didn't want to risk the torch bearer being accused of witchcraft by astonished locals seeing the flames.

HEARTS fans are still wallowing in their fine Scottish Cup win over Hibs. Whenever two Hearts fans are within earshot of a dejected Hibs fan, one will ask loudly: "What's the time?"

"Five past Hibs," his mate will eagerly reply.

IT WAS the final Celtic v Rangers game, which is why the chap in the pub announced: "The wife has to go into hospital for a small procedure, and she asked me to go with her. I told her it clashed with the Old Firm game, and she said, 'Can you not tape it?'

"I told her that was an excellent suggestion, but was she sure the hospital would allow her to take a camera and tripod in?"

THE OLYMPIC TORCH was paraded through Glasgow, and of course the occasion couldn't pass without some local rivalry. David Scott tells us: "As the Olympic Flame was run up Byres Road in Glasgow's West End, a group of topers abandoned Tennent's Bar to see the spectacle, with one asking, 'Where's it come fae?'

'Partick,' said another.

"'Partick? They're lucky they've still goat it.'"

Meanwhile the denizens of Partick are denying reports that some of their number were running alongside the Olympic flame trying to get a light for their fag.

FOLK are very practical in some parts of Scotland. A reader perusing the Raith Rovers v Partick Thistle football programme the other week read an interview with the previous winner of the 50/50 draw – a mainstay of small clubs' fundraising. The winner from Kirkcaldy was asked what he would do with his £479 win.

"I'll put it towards my fine," he replied.

WE WONDER if the BBC subtitles were trying to tell us something at Scotland's latest rugby international defeat when the commentator explained: "The Scottish pack are beginning to have difficulty coping with the pressure," but the subtitles stated: "The Scottish pack are beginning to have difficulty coping with depression."

SCOTLAND'S Six Nations match against England reminds a Bridge of Weir reader of a neighbour who attended a Scotland-France match and wanted to swap his Scotland top at the end with a chap wearing a French top.

Mustering all the schoolboy French he could remember, he stumbled his way through a request to swap jerseys, using a pitiful French accent for good measure.

"Get lost with yer lousy French accent," the chap replied. "I've just swapped this myself," replied a slightly aggrieved Scots punter.

THE CHELTENHAM Festival is one of the greatest weeks in horse racing. We recall the jovial chap at Cheltenham, enjoying a few pints of Guinness with his pals, who was approached by a down-at-heel character, hoping to scrounge a few bob, who whispered to him:

"Do you want the winner of the next race?" "No thanks," the chap boomed out in reply. "I've only got a small garden."

A READER tells us: "I had a few pals around for poker, and I said to the guy who won the most: how come you're lucky at cards, but you're so unlucky at picking winners at Cheltenham? 'I don't get to shuffle the horses,' he replied."

A WEST END reader attending a recent Partick Thistle match heard a young chap ask a scarf seller how much they were, and was told they were £7. "I'll give you a tenner for two of them," the fan then offered.

"This is Maryhill," the vendor replied. "No' the kasbah."

THE SCOTTISH Chess Championships took place in Glasgow's Trades Hall, with a £2,000 prize for the top player. It's a great game, chess, but alas, not everyone agrees. We remember comic Matt Kirshen at the Edinburgh Fringe declaring: "I was playing chess with my friend, and he said, 'Let's make this more interesting.' So we stopped playing chess."

THE SORRY plight of Rangers FC is creeping in everywhere. Russell Campbell was refereeing an eight-year-olds' football match when one of the lads went down, grazing his knee, and a parent shouted from the sidelines that it was a "terrible case of Rangers knee".

Says Russell: "After a short gap, he then added the explanation, 'totally skint.'"

AN AYRSHIRE reader tells us a truism he heard in his golf club the other day. A member at the bar declared: "Chaps who do imaginary golf swings in the office never break 100 on the course."

WE ARE trying not to intrude on the grief of Rangers Football Club, but reader John Jamieson in Ayr declares: "I understand one of Rangers' tax bills has risen to £15 million plus penalties. Typical, even the tax man is giving them penalties now."

"I MISSED the Oscars," said the Rangers fan in the pub the other night.

"But I'm assuming Craig Whyte didn't win the Best Director award."

ACTOR, and serial Burns-portrayer, John Cairney, tells in his book about his lifelong love affair with Celtic, *The Sevenpenny Gate*, of being Celtic's celebrity team-member on BBC sports quiz *Quizball*. There were graduates on the Celtic team, but Willie Wallace had to make up the numbers after someone called off.

Recalls John: "Wispy hadn't opened his mouth, so we arranged to leave one question to him. It was 'Who or what is a garryowen?' We all knew it was a kick from the hands to score in rugby, but looked at Wispy to respond.

"He gulped, pressed his buzzer, and whispered tentatively, 'The racing correspondent of the *Daily Record?*'"

TRADITIONALIST football fans, who like their players numbered from 1 to 11, will appreciate Clydebank comedian Kevin Bridges, at a football award ceremony, when he told Celtic striker Gary Hooper, who wears the number 88 on his jersey: "Gary, you have to make your mind up. Are you a football player or a bus?"

OUR TALES of cheap beer in Paisley remind entertainer Andy Cameron of when he worked in the crazy Rootes car factory in Linwood. Recalls Andy: "Big Hughie Campbell from Johnstone spent most of his day berating Paisley Buddies for being miserable.

"My favourite was his tale of the Paisley pub, when St Mirren won the Scottish Cup in 1959, selling drink at 1920 prices – the year the pub opened.

"There was a queue outside a mile long of Buddies although the pub was open. A stranger asked why they weren't taking up the offer, and was told, 'we're waiting for the happy hour.'"

READER Eddie Orme hears our favourite radio quote of the week when a Radio Scotland football commentator described a young, nervous footballer: "He's like a rabbit caught in the limelight."

PARTICK THISTLE held a special celebration at Hampden to mark the 40th anniversary of beating Celtic, who still had a number of Lisbon Lions playing for them, 4-1 in the League Cup final.

It was a glorious win, of course, but a little vignette we remember from that day – the Thistle team, followed by a camera crew, returned to their Firhill ground after the game to celebrate their win.

As the players stood outside Firhill it soon became apparent that no-one could find the key to let them in.

As one Jags player remarked: "I could have become a professional footballer or joined the circus. With Thistle you could do both."

SOME GOOD weather saw a rush for the golf courses as players try to fit in a few last rounds before the winter. One wise old player told us a truism about the game: "If your opponent has trouble remembering whether he took a six or a seven, he probably took eight."

HEARTS physio Alan Rae tells in his autobiography *Hands On Hearts*, that stocky midfielder Phil Stamp was walking his dog very early in the morning at Cramond. It leapt in the sea but was being pulled out by the strong tide. Phil jumped in and swam out to save him.

Recalls Alan: "Soaked through, he staggered back to the main road to hail a taxi.

"One eventually stopped, offering salvation until the cabbie recognised who he was. 'You're Phil Stamp. You scored against the Hibs . . . you can walk!'"

SRU president Ian McLauchlin, doing some Ayrshire reminiscing at Cumnock Rugby Club's 50th anniversary dinner, recalled that during a rugby tour of New Zealand while the other players were moaning about having to stay in a one-horse town in the middle of nowhere, Ian piped up that compared to his home village of Tarbolton, the New Zealand place wasn't too bad.

ENGLAND didn't do too well in the European Championships. It was best summed up by a reader who said: "The England football team are like a holiday romance. Every time you fool yourself that it will last longer than two weeks – but it never does."